Sports Law in Japan

Sports Law in Japan

Fourth Edition

Takuya Yamazaki

This book was originally published as a monograph in the International Encyclopaedia of Laws/Sports Law.

Founding Editor: Roger Blanpain
General Editor: Frank Hendrickx
Volume Editor: Michele Colucci

Wolters Kluwer

Published by:
Kluwer Law International B.V.
PO Box 316
2400 AH Alphen aan den Rijn
The Netherlands
E-mail: lrs-sales@wolterskluwer.com
Website: www.wolterskluwer.com/en/solutions/kluwerlawinternational

Sold and distributed by:
Wolters Kluwer Legal & Regulatory U.S.
7201 McKinney Circle
Frederick, MD 21704
United States of America
E-mail: customer.service@wolterskluwer.com

ISBN 978-94-035-4891-3

e-Book: ISBN 978-94-035-4652-0
web-PDF: ISBN 978-94-035-4413-7

The Author

Takuya Yamazaki gained his LLB from Waseda University (Tokyo, Japan) in 1993. He then qualified as an attorney-at-law in Japan and was admitted into the Dai-Ni Tokyo Bar Association in 1997. Takuya has vast legal experience, initially working for Max Law Offices in Tokyo from 1997 until 2000. Subsequently, in 2001, he founded Field-R Law Offices, a specialized sports and entertainment law practice based in Tokyo, where he currently serves as the Founding Partner.

Takuya holds a number of executive positions in international and domestic sports organizations, including CAS arbitrator, Chairman of FIFPro Asia/Oceania, board member of the World Players Association, advisory panel member in the Grievance Mechanism for the Tokyo 2020 Sustainable Sourcing Code, and board member of the Japan Sports Law Association. He has also served as a member of the FIFA Dispute Resolution Chamber (2009–2019) and a member of special committees of sports organizations, such as Japan Sports Arbitration Agency, Tokyo 2020 Olympics and Paralympics Organizing Committee, and Japan Sports Association.

Takuya has received the following honours and recognition. He was selected by 'Best Lawyers International' consecutively from 2009 until now as one of the 'Best Lawyers' in the fields of 'Media and Entertainment Law' and 'Sports' in Japan (http://www.bestlawyers.com/), selected on 29 August 2009 'High-Flying Corporate Lawyers' edition of the acclaimed *Shukan Diamond* Magazine as one of the two 'Brilliant Lawyers That Can Really Deliver Results' in the field of entertainment and sports laws.

He has also given many lectures and presentations at major international conferences. His major lectures, presentations and publications can be found at http://www.field-r.com.

The Author

Table of Contents

The Author 3

List of Abbreviations 11

Acknowledgements 13

General Introduction 15

Chapter 1. General Background 15

§1. School Sports System, the Corporate Sports System and the Professional Sports System 15

§2. The Present Situation Concerning the School Sports System in Japan 15

§3. Present Situation Concerning the Corporate Sports System in Japan 16

§4. Present Situation Concerning the Professional Sports System in Japan 17

Chapter 2. Sources of Sports Law 18

§1. History of the Study of Sports Law in Japan 18

§2. Basic Sports Act and the Debate about Sports Rights 18

§3. The BSA as an Amendatory Law to the SPA 20

Chapter 3. Specificity of Sports 22

§1. The Rule of Law and the Autonomy of Sports Associations 22

§2. Reasons Why Sports Rights Are Required 24

Part I. Organization of Sport 27

Table of Contents

Chapter 1. Sports Governance 27

§1. Governmental Institutions and Bodies 27

§2. National Olympic Committee and Sports Associations 28

Chapter 2. Public Regulation 31

§1. Fundamental Rights 31
I. Image Rights 31
II. Image Rights in Baseball 32
III. Image Rights in Football 33

§2. Governmental Conditions and Permits 34
I. Issues Concerning the Eligibility of Foreigners to Participate in Sports 34
A. Introduction 34
B. Cases in Relation to Amateur Sports 34
C. Cases in Relation to Professional Sports 35
D. Nippon Professional Baseball 35
E. Professional Football 36
II. Issues Concerning the Eligibility of Females to Participate in Sports 37

§3. Tort Law 37
I. Legal Responsibility in Sports 37
II. Sports Competitors and Tort Law 39
A. Liability and Negligence of Competitors in Sports Accidents 39
B. Liability and Illegality of Competitors in Sports Accidents 39
C. Liability and Capacity to Assume Liability of Competitors in Sports Accidents 40
III. Sports Coaches and Instructors and Tort Law 40
IV. Sport Facility Managers and Administrators and Tort 41
V. Validity of Waiver Forms 42
VI. Damages and Partial Negligence 42
VII. Insurance Systems 43
VIII. Other Cases of Tortious Liability in Relation to Sport 43
IX. Illegal Gambling and Match-Fixing 43
A. Legal System Governing Betting and Lotteries in Japan 44
B. Special Laws Governing Public Gambling 46
1. Horse Racing 46
2. Bicycle Racing (Keirin) 47
3. Motorbike Racing 47
4. Motorboat Racing 48
X. Football Betting as a Means of Promoting the Sport 48
XI. Match-Fixing in Japan 50
A. Black Mist Scandal in Professional Baseball 50

B. Match-Fixing in Motorbike Racing and Horse Racing 51
C. Match-Fixing in Sumo Wrestling 51
D. Illegal Betting in Professional Baseball 52
E. Illegal Betting in Badminton 52

§4. TAX 53

§5. SPORTS JUSTICE 53
I. Legal Basis for Justice in Sports 53
II. Sports Disputes and the Necessity for Alternative Dispute Resolution 55
A. Establishment of the JSAA 57
B. Arbitrations and Mediations Handled by the JSAA 57
1. Disputes Adjudicated by an Arbitration Panel Using Sports Arbitration Rules 58
2. Arbitration under Sports Arbitration Rules Based on a Specific Arbitration Agreement 58
3. Mediation under Sports Mediation Rules Based on a Specific Mediation Agreement 59
4. Arbitration under Sports Arbitration Rules for Doping Disputes 59
5. Arbitrations under Sports Arbitration Rules for Member Associations 60
C. Limits of the JSAA 60

Part II. Sport and Employment 63

Chapter 1. General Issues 63

§1. AMATEURISM AND ELIGIBILITY ISSUES 63

§2. STUDENT ATHLETES ISSUES 65
I. High School Baseball Scholarship Issue and the JSBC 65
II. Wide-Ranging Revisions to the JSBC and New Developments Concerning the School Sports System and Amateurism 66
III. Handling of Collective Responsibility 67
IV. Legal Position of Student Athletes 68

§3. ISSUES CONCERNING SEMI-PROFESSIONAL ATHLETES 68
I. Issues Concerning the Position of Athletes in the Corporate Sports System 68
II. Issues Concerning Restrictions on Player Transfers 71
III. Issues Concerning the Contracts of Coaches and Managers 72

Chapter 2. Sources of Employment Law 73

§1. Legal Status of Players 73
I. Professional Sports Players and Athletes as Workers 73
II. 'Workers' under the LUA and Professional Sports Players and Athletes 73
III. 'Workers' under the LSA and the IACIA and Professional Sports Players and Athletes 74

§2. Employment Relationship 75

§3. Fundamental Rights and Obligations for Clubs and Players 76
I. Baseball 76
A. System Based on the American Model of Baseball 76
B. Restrictions on Rookies Entering Clubs: The Amateur Draft and Related Matters 76
C. Transfer Restrictions 79
1. Reserve System 79
2. Issues Concerning Foreign Transfers: The Posting System and Related Matters 81
3. Trade System 84
II. Football 85
A. Transfer Restrictions 85
III. Basketball: B-League 86
IV. Boxing 87

§4. Agents' Regulations 87
I. Situation Concerning the Player Agent and Management Business and Related Contracts 87
II. Contents of the Agent and Management Service Business and the Agent System 89
III. Actual Practice in Baseball 91
IV. Actual Practice in Football 92

§5. Employment and Economic Dispute Settlement 93
I. Baseball 93
II. Football 93

§6. Social Security 95

§7. Tax Law 96

Part III. Doping and Sport 99

Chapter 1. General Issues 99

Chapter 2. Public Regulation 101

Chapter 3. Private Regulation 102

Part IV. Sport and Commerce 105

Chapter 1. General Issues 105

§1. INTRODUCTION 105

§2. HOSTING AND PROMOTING EVENTS 107
I. Types of Events and the Legal Status of the Promotion Rights 107
II. Various Contracts Involved with Hosting and Promoting Events 108
A. Contracts Concerning Contents 108
B. Contracts Concerning Venues 108
C. Contracts Concerning Money (Capital) 109
D. Other Contracts in Connection with Hosting and Promoting Events (Promotion Revenue Contracts) 110

Chapter 2. Public Regulation 111

§1. MEDIA AND TELEVISION RIGHTS 111
I. Legal Scope and Limits of Broadcasting Rights 111
II. Broadcasting Rights Contracts 112
III. Internet Broadcast Rights 113

§2. SPONSORING 114
I. Legal Basis and Limits of Sponsorship Rights 114
II. Players' Image Rights and Endorsement Contracts 114

§3. MERCHANDISING 115
I. Legal Basis for Merchandising Rights 115
II. Legal Basis for Use of the Images of Players and Athletes in the Merchandising Business 117

§4. OWNERSHIP OF CLUBS 118

Chapter 3. Competition Law 119

§1. SPORTS AND THE APPLICATION OF COMPETITION LAW 119

§2. PROFESSIONAL BASEBALL DRAFT SYSTEM AND RESERVE SYSTEM UNDER COMPETITION LAW 121

§3. Restrictions Concerning the Entry of New Teams to the NPB and Competition Law 121

§4. Issues Concerning Professional Baseball Players' Image Rights and Competition Law 122

§5. Antitrust Issues Relating to Consumption Tax on Pro-baseball Player Compensation 123

§6. Other Issues 123

Chapter 4. COVID-19 and Its Impact on National Sports 125

§1. Impact 125

§2. Measures 125

Chapter 5. Tokyo 2020 Olympics and Paralympics 127

§1. 'Unity in Diversity' and Human Rights 127

§2. COVID-19 – Laws and the 'Playbook' 128

§3. New Legislation Regarding Tokyo 2020 129

Selected Bibliography 131

Index 135

List of Abbreviations

ADR	Alternative Dispute Resolution
BSA	Basic Sports Act
CAS	Court of Arbitration for Sport
DPJ	Democratic Party of Japan
FIBA	International Basketball Federation
FIFA	*Fédération Internationale de Football Association* French for International Federation of Association Football
FIFPro	World Players' Union: The Worldwide Representative Organization for All Professional Football Players
HRA	Horse Racing Act
IACIA	Industrial Accident Compensation Insurance Act
IOC	International Olympic Committee
ITA	Income Tax Act
JABA	Japan Amateur Baseball Association
JADA	Japan Anti-Doping Agency
JBA	Japan Basketball Association
JFA	Japan Football Association
JFTC	Japan Fair Trade Commission
JOC	Japan Olympic Committee
JPBPA	Japan Professional Baseball Players Association
JPC	Japanese Paralympic Committee
JPFA	Japan Pro-Footballers Association
JPSA	Japan Para-Sports Association
JSA	Japan Sumo Association
JSAA	Japan Sports Arbitration Agency
JSBC	Japan Student Baseball Charter
JSC	Japan Sport Council
JSF	Japan Swimming Federation
JSPO	Japan Sports Association
JTL	Japan Top League

List of Abbreviations

KBO	Korea Baseball Organization
LCA	Labour Contracts Act
LDP	Liberal Democratic Party
LSA	Labour Standards Act
LUA	Labour Union Act
MboatRA	Motorboat Racing Act
METI	Ministry of Economy, Trade and Industry
MEXT	Ministry of Education, Culture, Sports, Science and Technology
MHLW	Ministry of Health, Labour and Welfare
MLB	Major League Baseball
MLBPA	Major League Baseball Players Association
MRA	Motorbike Racing Act
MWA	Minimum Wages Act
NDRC	National Dispute Resolution Chambers
NFL	National Football League
NPB	Nippon Professional Baseball
NFLP	NFL Properties
NPO	Non-Profit Organization
SEA	School Education Act
SPA	Sports Promotion Act
SPLA	Sports Promotion Lottery Act
SRA	State Redress Act
TLRC	Tokyo Labour Relations Commission
TOCOG	Tokyo 2020 Olympics and Paralympics Organizing Committee
TUE	Therapeutic Use Exemption
UCPA	Unfair Competition Prevention Act
UNESCO	United Nations Educational Scientific and Cultural Organization
WADA	World Anti-Doping Agency

Acknowledgements

To begin, I am profoundly grateful to Dr Roger Blanpain, Dr Michele Colucci and Dr Frank Hendrickx for providing me with this great opportunity to write about sports law in Japan.

Personally, being given this chance has enabled me to fully utilize my experience as a sports lawyer, in order to examine the current situation of Japanese sports law, and also to consider its future course. It has been a thoroughly beneficial experience.

Up until now, I have had many chances to give speeches and presentations on the state of sports law in Japan. Nevertheless, this is the first time I have been able to present an overall, comprehensive assessment of Japanese sports law in the form of a monograph.

From this point forward, it is my desire to continue being active in this field so that more people can get to know about the situation in Japanese sports law.

In order to assist you in understanding this monograph, you should be aware that Japanese sports law is still in the process of developing. However, having said that, it is now at a stage where it can prosper and flourish in the future. For instance, the historic Basic Sports Act came into force in 2011. There is a positive realization that this legislation marks a significant step in the right direction for Japanese sports law.

This project has been both challenging and exciting to work on given the complex legal areas it covers. It is my sincere hope that this monograph will be consulted by many people who are interested in Japanese sports law. Plus, even if only a little, it can contribute to developments in this field.

In completing this project, first and foremost, I would like to thank my invaluable paralegal, Andrew Hall, for his substantial contributions. Had I not met someone with his brilliance and eagerness, it would not have been possible to complete this project. I would also like to express my sincere gratitude to my assistant Mami Ishihara whose continued support has been indispensable to me for many years.

I feel blessed to pursue my career as a sports lawyer, which is undoubtedly a challenging and difficult field but thoroughly satisfying. Moreover, I am able to accomplish this work because of the trust placed in me by my clients (including many famous Japanese sports stars), my reliable partners, colleagues, and staff at Field-R Law Offices and also my family. This monograph is a token of my gratitude to all those who have supported my efforts, and a testament to my commitment and determination to constantly improve myself as a sports lawyer.

Acknowledgements

This monograph was last updated in July 2017. I would like to thank my colleague Nan Sato for her invaluable assistance with updating the contents of this monograph.

Sadly, Dr Roger Blanpain, who has inspired many in the fields of labour law and sports law, is no longer with us at the time of this update. However, the unparalleled legacies that he left behind will be carried on.

General Introduction

Chapter 1. General Background

§1. School Sports System, the Corporate Sports System and the Professional Sports System

1. With Japanese sports, amateurism was long held in high esteem as it had been central to the development of both the school sports and corporate sports systems. Professional sports in Japan, until the birth of the J-League in 1993, existed with baseball as the only professional league. However, since the inception of the J-League, professional baseball and football have become the two most popular sports. Also, in recent years, with the development from the *corporate sports system* to the *club sports system*, yet greater numbers of corporate sports clubs are turning professional. This is illustrated by the emergence of the new basketball league B.League.[1] The following is an overview of the present situation for sports in Japan in relation to:

– the school sports system;
– the corporate sports system; and
– the professional sports system.

§2. The Present Situation Concerning the School Sports System in Japan

2. Since the Meiji era, sports in Japan have been led by the school sports system. As a result, nowadays, the school sports system still plays an important function in cultivating young sports players and athletes.

3. High school baseball is integral to the game as a whole in Japan, in particular, with the long-running national high school tournament called *Koshien*. This tournament is the preeminent and massively popular sporting event in the Japanese amateur sports calendar.

4. The same system has also become apparent in football with high schools and universities being invaluable suppliers of players to the J-League. Even after the

1. The website is available at: http://www.bleague.jp.

emergence of youth academies of J-League clubs, the school sports system, like with baseball, is still important in football, particularly in connection with the *Koshien*-style national school football tournament.

5. In schools, many sports clubs exist, such as baseball, football, tennis, table tennis, basketball, volleyball and track and field. These sports have played an important role in the school sports system. However, in the case of sports which many schools have not established clubs for, including golf, swimming, figure-skating, gymnastics, judo and sumo wrestling, such sports have conventionally been considered as *extracurricular*. Thus, it can be said that the school sports system plays a primary role in the development of sports in Japan. Nevertheless, the club sports system has been playing its role in relation to the demands of sports which are not covered by the school sports system.

§3. Present Situation Concerning the Corporate Sports System in Japan

6. In the period of rapid economic growth (from the 1960s to 1980s), the so-called *corporate sports system* became an inherent part of sports in Japan. A clear example of this was the powerhouse Nippon Steel Corporation Rugby Club in Kamaishi (Iwate Prefecture) that made rugby ubiquitous within the region's sporting culture.[2]

7. In recent years, corporate sports clubs that previously, at the least in the eyes of the public, operated as amateurs have gradually changed to carry out their activities on a professional basis. For example, there has been an increase in the cases where players have actually entered into contracts in their capacity as *professional players* and not as *employees*.[3] The same kinds of developments have also been occurring with some of the leagues themselves becoming professional. One particular example of this is basketball with the B.League that started in 2016.

8. In 2005, many of Japan's ball sports leagues, in order not only to facilitate the sharing of such know-how for their mutual development but also to enhance their international competitiveness, established the Japan Top League (JTL).[4] Presently the JTL boasts a membership of twelve sports leagues (not only limited to non-professional leagues), including football (men's and women's), rugby, basketball (men's and women's), volleyball, handball, ice hockey, field hockey, softball, futsal and American football.

---

2. Please note that the Nippon Steel Corporation Kamaishi Rugby Team was disbanded in 2001 due to economic constraints. However, the team was re-established in the same year as the independent Kamaishi Sea Waves Rugby Football Club. The Japanese website is available at: http://www.kamaishi-seawaves.com/.
3. Sasakawa Sports Foundation, *Sports Paper: The Future Direction for Sports* 129 (Sasakawa Sports Foundation, 2011).
4. The JTL website is available at http://www.japantopleague.jp/.

§4. PRESENT SITUATION CONCERNING THE PROFESSIONAL SPORTS SYSTEM IN JAPAN

9. In terms of professional sport, baseball is Japan's most popular sport with the longest history. Apart from this, Japan's national sport of sumo wrestling has been run for many years with the sense that it is a professional sport. Nevertheless, sumo is still regarded in character as a traditional sport, which is very insular and bound by many old customs.

10. In 1993, J-League football emerged to join baseball as another professional sport. At present, in Japan, baseball and football have acquired the status of the two most popular professional sports leagues. In addition, various independent sports leagues have also been established: including the B.League (basketball) and the independent baseball leagues such as Island League in Shikoku and Kyushu, the Baseball Challenge League, and the Kansai Independent Baseball League. Furthermore, to strengthen the Japanese national rugby team for the 2019 Rugby World Cup, the Japanese team of Sunwolves participated in the southern hemisphere professional league of Super Rugby from 2016 until 2020. From September 2021, WE. League, the first professional league of women's football has started.

11. Apart from those mentioned above, other professional sports exist in Japan, such as boxing and golf. On top of this, there is also a group of professional sports operated for the purpose of publicly managed gambling in the form of horse racing, bicycle racing (keirin), motorboat racing and motorbike racing. There is an association named Japan Professional Sports Association which has some of the professional sports associations as its members.[5]

5. The Japan Professional Sports Association's website in Japanese is available at: http://www.jpsa.jp/index.html.

Chapter 2. Sources of Sports Law

§1. History of the Study of Sports Law in Japan

12. Historically, the study of sports law in Japan centred on the debate in relation to the legal accountability for sports accidents.[6] Not surprisingly, due to a competitor's carelessness, incidents such as collisions with opponents and the use of defective equipment can result in serious injuries or even death in sports. On the grounds that such cases occurred within sports, these were usually dealt with internally as the self-responsibility of the parties concerned. However, as this process alone does not produce adequate solutions, in the pursuit of accountability there are instances where the parties concerned have been to court. In fact, since before the Second World War, there was an accumulation of many such legal judgments.[7]

13. As sports developed after the war, the instances of sports-related accidents continued to increase. The study of sports law then became concentrated on the accidents in the school sports system. Even in professional sports, particularly baseball, the so-called *Egawa Incident*,[8] concerning the draft system depriving players of the freedom to join teams, occurred in 1978. This gradually brought about recognition of sporting legal issues, including debate on the human rights of players.

14. Furthermore, in Japan, many amateur sports tournaments developed through both the *school* and *corporate sports* systems. In order to attract the best athletes, it became an accepted practice for schools, companies or prefectures that hosted or joined these tournaments to prepare special contracts, financial incentives and high prize money. This fostered debate about whether such practices constituted a violation of *amateurism*.

§2. Basic Sports Act and the Debate about Sports Rights

15. Up until the adoption of the Basic Sports Act (BSA) in 2011,[9] the Sports Promotion Act (SPA), which was enacted in 1961, three years before the Tokyo Olympics, was the only stand-alone legislation for sports in Japan.[10] The objective of the

6. Masaji Chiba & Yoshio Hamano (eds), *An Introduction to Sports Law* 11 (Taiiku Shisetsu Shuppan Ltd., December 1995).
7. *Ibid.*
8. There were a series of incidents concerning the player Suguru Egawa in relation to his contract with the Central League's Yomiuri Giants before the 1978 draft. Under the draft system, new players could not freely negotiate with all the professional teams; they could only talk to teams who had won the right in a lottery at the draft. The Giants, who desperately wanted to sign Egawa, used an interpretation of a loophole in the Nippon Professional Baseball Agreement to force through a contract with Egawa one day before the 1978 draft. The Giants were massively criticized by other teams and the public.
9. *Basic Sports Act*, law no. 78 of 2011.
10. *Sports Promotion Act*, law no. 141 of 1961 and amendment law no. 97 of 1997.

SPA was defined in Article 1(1) as, 'to articulate fundamental policies for the promotion of sports in Japan, which shall ensure the sound development of the peoples' minds and bodies, while also contributing to bright and prosperous lives for the people'. Article 1(2) stated that '[t]he operation of this law to make sports compulsory for the people … is forbidden'.

16. The SPA defined measures for the promotion of sports by public administration bodies. Thus, it was not established based on the human rights viewpoint of the parties connected with sports. The SPA contained no such provisions. Accordingly, from the perspective of the so-called *rule of law* in sports (including, the human rights of athletes and players, fairness, impartiality, due process, maintaining the governance of sports associations, and ensuring thorough compliance), the enactment of the BSA was long called for.

17. In July 2009, the congress of the then-ruling Liberal Democratic Party (LDP) and Komeito Party (Komeito) proposed a bill in the Japanese parliament for the BSA, which was intended to radically overhaul the SPA. However, the Democratic Party of Japan (DPJ), which came to power just two months later, strongly opposed and scrapped the BSA bill. One main reason for this DPJ opposition was that the LDP/Komeito sponsored a bill that in no way incorporated the notion of *sports rights*.

18. Even following this, a lengthy debate ensued about the BSA until it was finally enacted in June 2011 under the DPJ administration (there will be an examination of the BSA below). However, it should be noted that in the preamble and Article 2 of the Act, the idea is clearly stated that 'all people have the right to maintain a wholesome and happy lifestyle through the participation in sports'.

19. Among sports law scholars in Japan, human rights for sports participants have long been debated as an interpretation of the present Constitution. Over time, this has developed as an argument that all people are entitled to *sports rights*. In other words, the *sports rights* debate has evolved.[11]

20. Prior to the adoption by the twentieth United Nations Educational Scientific and Cultural Organization (UNESCO) General Assembly in November 1978 of the 'International Charter of Physical Education and Sport', in Japan debate had already begun that *sports rights* must be fully embraced. The bases for this, in the sense of the freedom to play sports, are contained in Article 13 (the right to pursue happiness)[12] and Article 25 (minimum standards of wholesome and cultured living) of the

11. Masaru Ogasawara (ed.) et al., *An Introductory Dialogue to Sports Jurisprudence* 30 (2nd ed., Fumashoubo Ltd., April 2007).
12. *The Constitution of Japan*, Art. 13 states, 'All of the people shall be respected as individuals. Their right to life, liberty, and the pursuit of happiness shall, to the extent that it does not interfere with the public welfare, be the supreme consideration in legislation and in other governmental affairs.'

Constitution of Japan.[13] More specifically, the text of Article 25 is the basis for guarantees that the state shall provide social rights for the people, including establishing the facilities necessary for participating in sports.

21. Furthermore, Article 1 of the Basic Education Act contains provisions relating to the *cultivation of peoples' health both mentally and physically.*[14] The bases for such educational objectives, in the sense of the right to sports/physical education, are guaranteed in Article 26 of the Constitution.[15] In any event, from a long time ago, the concept that human rights in sports must be constitutionally guaranteed has been actively pursued within Japan's sports legal research field. In 1997, the Japan Sports Law Association published a draft BSA bill, which has *sports rights* as its core concept.

22. Under the DPJ administration, in August 2010, the Ministry of Education, Culture, Sports, Science, and Technology (MEXT) announced its 'Strategy for Sports Nation' policy,[16] which also expressed the necessity of bringing the BSA into force. Along with this, the policy also stressed the necessity of securing ideals in the sports world, including a greater level of transparency and fairness. It is against this background that the concept of *sports rights* was incorporated into the BSA.

§3. The BSA as an Amendatory Law to the SPA

23. As aforementioned, in the period prior to the establishment of the BSA, Japan's main statute for sports was the 1961 formulated SPA. After fifty years, the SPA underwent a full-fledged revision in the form of the 2011 BSA. The main difference between the two acts is that the BSA was established on the premise of *sports rights.* Namely, a key concept of the BSA is that *all people have the right to maintain a wholesome and happy lifestyle through participation in sports.*

24. In order to guarantee these *sports rights*, many questions arise as to what obligations the State and regional/prefectural bodies take on, as well as what actions the sports associations can themselves undertake. Thus, the BSA now focuses on the corresponding regulations of these bodies. This is in pure contrast to the SPA which largely focused on the promotion of sports through government.

13. *The Constitution of Japan*, Art. 25 states: All people shall have the right to maintain the minimum standards of wholesome and cultured living. In all spheres of life, the State shall use its endeavours for the promotion and extension of social welfare and security, and of public health.
14. *Basic Education Act*, law no. 120 of 2006.
15. *The Constitution of Japan*, Art. 26 states: All people shall have the right to receive an equal education correspondent to their ability, as provided by law. All people shall be obligated to have all boys and girls under their protection receive ordinary education as provided for by law. Such compulsory education shall be free.
16. MEXT, *Strategy for Sports Nation* (MEXT 2010), this is available in English at: https://www.mext.go.jp/en/policy/sports/lawandplan/title02/detail02/sdetail02/1374143.htm.

25. Article 1 of the BSA stipulates the legal purpose of the Act, with Article 2 covering the basic principles. Articles 3–8 oblige the State and regional/prefectural public bodies to further these principles, as well as provide similar requirements in relation to the initiatives of sports associations. Articles 9 and 10 also lay out that the State and regional/prefectural public bodies should implement initiatives for the promotion of sport based on the principles in Article 2.

26. In relation to formulating basic measures for sports, the Act stipulates the following provisions for the state and regional/prefectural public bodies:

- basic Conditions for Equipment and Facilities (Articles 11–20);
- promotion of Regional Sports (Articles 21–24); and
- promotion of Competitive Sports (Articles 25–29).

27. Furthermore, Articles 30–32 oblige the state and regional/prefectural public bodies to establish systems in relation to the promotion of sports (including the duty of the state to set up a Sports Promotion Council). The financial supports by the state and regional/prefectural public bodies to achieve these aims are regulated by Articles 32–35.

Chapter 3. Specificity of Sports

§1. The Rule of Law and the Autonomy of Sports Associations

28. In the debate on the Japanese Constitutional Law, the special society of sport is termed *partial society*. To a certain extent, the freedom of the sports associations in this 'partial society' is recognized in laws. On the other hand, under the constitutional *rule of law*, there are limits on this autonomy. In fact, as awareness has grown that sports associations may act beyond their autonomy, much legal debate has ensued about whether in such cases these associations should be subject to the regulations in accordance with national and statutory law.

29. For example, in general society, if somebody committed violent and injurious acts which are associated with boxing, it is highly likely that that person would be subject to sanctions under the penal and civil codes. However, in the special world of boxing, such conduct is legitimized so long as the aggrieved party consents to it under certain rules stipulated for sporting competitions. For all types of sports associations, the right to enact such rules and regulations is derived from the *freedom of assembly and association provisions* contained in Article 21 of the Constitution of Japan. Furthermore, based on this article, the freedom to enact disciplinary rules, including penalties, is guaranteed.[17]

30. Even within this special society of sports in Japan, the Constitution is the highest system of national law. Therefore, in relation to conduct that excessively limits human rights or that goes beyond the guaranteed autonomy of sports associations, it becomes necessary to exercise regulations by national law.

31. Historically, in Japan, sports was recognized as physical education, unlike in Europe and America where it was seen as leisure. Thus, in Japan, sports were often practised based on the hierarchical relationship between teacher and student. This relationship is also rooted in the Confucius culture and the samurai spirit, with the rule that it is essential to respect one's superiors. Within this system of superiority, it is easy for instructors to go too far in keenly instructing their students (referred to as *Shigoki*) which has resulted in cases of human rights violations, such as injury causing death[18] and excessive corporal punishment.

---

17. The *Constitution of Japan*, Art. 21 states, 'Freedom of assembly and association as well as speech, press and all other forms of expression are guaranteed. 2) No censorship shall be maintained, nor shall the secrecy of any means of communication be violated.'
18. *Tokitaizan* Death: On 26 Jul. 2007, *Tokitaizan*, a young wrestler of the *Tokitsukaze* sumo stable, died from multiple traumatic shocks. In relation to this tragic incident, the stable master and three senior wrestlers were prosecuted with the crime of injury causing death (manslaughter). The court handed down a guilty verdict with a suspended sentence to the three wrestlers. The stable master received a prison sentence without suspension. The court noted that, 'The wrestler was forced to train in an exceptionally long sparring session, at which he was brutally beaten, including being smashed with a metal bat and repeatedly punched and kicked in the sumo training ring' (author's translation from Japanese). Nagoya District Court Judgment, 29 May 2009.

32. According to the MEXT report 'The Position Regarding Disciplinary Action against Educators in 2008', in 2008 for acts of corporal punishment: 140 educators (an increase of 16 from the previous year) were subject to disciplinary action; and 376 educators (a rise of 5 from the previous year) were subject to disciplinary action, including warnings. Out of the 376 educators, 58 were subject to the said disciplinary action, including warnings for acts of corporal punishment committed during 'after school club activities' held at 'sports grounds and gymnasiums'.[19]

33. Corporal punishment in sports lasted for a long time, during which it was extremely difficult for players to raise the issue. However, a scandal that happened in 2013 drastically changed the situation, and since then, there has been a strong movement to eliminate corporal punishment in sports in Japan. In January 2013, fifteen Japanese female judokas, including London Olympic judokas, brought accusations of ongoing corporal punishment against their head coach. This incident was treated with fury by the Japanese mass media and became a big scandal. Against the background of these accusations, was another tragic incident that occurred prior to this in December 2012, namely, the suicide of a second-year student (17 years old) who belonged to the basketball club of Sakuranomiya Senior High School in Osaka, following repeated corporal punishment by his coach. Accusations of this corporal punishment arose from a suicide note left by the student. As a result of this turmoil, the head coach of the women judo's team was forced to take responsibility by resigning, and Sakuranomiya Senior High School's basketball coach was subject to a disciplinary dismissal. For Japan, with Tokyo bidding to host the 2020 Olympics, these incidents have had a massive impact; Japan's media has heavily rebuked the governing structure of Japan's sports which had for a long time done nothing to remedy such situations. This then prompted Japan's MEXT in a press conference on 5 February 2013 to call for the eradication of violence in sports instruction and state that, 'This is the biggest crisis in the history of Japanese sport.' The Diet Members Federation for Sports also began reforming the content of relevant laws, including allowing for the establishment of a third-party body to counsel afflicted athletes and to apply appropriate corrective measures. Moreover, there have been other positive developments in eradicating violence in sports, such as the establishment of grievance consultation mechanisms by the Japan Olympic Committee (JOC), the Japan Sports Association (JSPO), and the Japan Football Association (JFA).

34. Also from this superiority system, athletes could not object to the actions of these *superiors* even though they excessively restricted human rights. Thus, human rights continued to be widely restricted as often nobody could voice their opinions (for athletes, objecting was seen as a protest against authority, and as such, they risked their sporting activities being discontinued). Correspondingly, even if such issues occurred, they were frequently dealt with internally by the sports world.

19. Tokyo: MEXT, 1 Apr. 2009. The report is available in Japanese at: http://www.mext.go.jp/a_menu/shotou/jinji/1288132.htm.

Given the small possibility that sports disputes were resolved using legal dispute resolution mechanisms, few instances of human rights violations in sports were unmasked.[20]

35. Sports law has an important mission in protecting players and athletes in a weak position, including from having their human rights infringed by the sports associations. The role of sports law has, therefore, become significant in realizing a balance between guaranteeing the autonomy of sports associations and the *rule of law*. Within the *partial society* of sports, in terms of respecting the autonomy of sports associations to resolve disputes internally, there is a legal theory that such disputes shall be beyond judicial review as far as it does not affect the civil law order and the whole Japanese legal systems under the Constitution. This is generally termed the *partial society theory,* which has been accepted in judgments of the Supreme Court of Japan.[21]

36. However, under this theory, it becomes a difficult problem to judge what actually constitutes an internal dispute within such *partial societies* (sports associations). Therefore, when courts need to determine whether they have jurisdiction to hear such disputes, the general interpretation is that they should positively take judicial review if the relevant association's internal regulations and conduct infringe any rights guaranteed by the Constitution.[22]

§2. Reasons Why Sports Rights Are Required

37. Due to the particularities within the *partial society* of sport, there is a need for autonomous and internal sport-specific regulations within these sports societies. Contrary to this, however, the situation has arisen that such autonomous regulations can easily violate human rights. This is why the concept of *sports rights* is strongly needed.

38. In Japan, such *sports rights* are not directly recognized in legal judgments.[23] Nevertheless, there are several situations which serve to illustrate where the concept of *sports rights* is needed. For instance, in the school sports system, it was frequently the case that where one member of a team was involved in a scandal or

20. Masato Dougauchi & Yoshihisa Hayakawa (eds), *An Introduction to Sports Law* 92 (Minerva Shobou Ltd., April 2011).
21. Supreme Court of Japan Judgment, 19 Oct. 1960, Supreme Court of Japan, Civil Decisions Reporter (*Minshu*), vol. 14, no. 12, 2633.
22. Tokyo District Court Judgment, 2 Feb. 1988, Decision Times (*Hanrei Taimuzu*) no. 663, 230. Please also *see* para. 202 for more detail.
23. However, there are examples of such *sports rights* cases going to trial. For instance, this occurred when a rubber baseball team based in Tokyo participated in an amateur baseball tournament hosted by parties, including media broadcasters. The Japan Rubber Baseball Association then suspended the team from participating in all other tournaments for one year, as the team's participation in the tournament violated the Association's regulations, which states, 'Regular team members … cannot participate in any tournaments that are hosted for the purpose of seeking commercial, advertising, political and any other gains' (author's translation from Japanese). Following this, the team brought

guilty of some misconduct, not only was that member but the whole team was subject to disciplinary action, such as being suspended from sports tournaments.

39. Even in March 2009, when it was discovered that a member of the Nippon Sports Science University men's athletics team (jumping events) had been using cannabis, all forty-six athletes in the jumping events team received indefinite competition suspensions, and the whole track and field team were suspended for five days. In addition, the Inter-University Athletic Union of Kanto, on top of suspending the university's track and field team for three months, withdrew the team's nomination for the *Izumo Ekiden* (a road relay race) and deprived it of its seeding for the *Hakone Ekiden.*

40. The imposition of these sanctions for the team members who did not commit any misconduct was based on *collective responsibility*. Thus, it can be said that these team members had their right to self-determination violated. Generally, in the sports world, despite the fact that athletes are subject to such inequitable rulings, it is seldom the case that such rulings are challenged through legal means, including lawsuits.[24] This is said to be one example where the sports world does not come under the rule of law.

41. Another example of this was in June 2009, when regarding the arrest of two members of Kinki University's boxing team on suspicion of robbery, the university made the team accountable for the matter by disbanding it. This is an issue which must be debated, as the athletes who were not connected to the alleged robbery were stripped of their sporting rights.

42. In particular, among competitive sports, the aforesaid hierarchical system exists within clubs and associations (in the form of trainers and athletes, educators and students and seniors and juniors) where it is demanded that participants endure strict training and perform at highly competitive levels. In these hierarchical systems, it is difficult for players and athletes to voice their opinions. Therefore, simply due to the nature of these systems, even if rights violations occur, it is hard to unmask the true situation.

43. Overall, it is difficult to say in the first place that sports are influenced by the *rule of law*. Thus, there is a substantial need to establish this within the sports world. Herein lay the reasons why *sports rights* are required.

---

a case to Tokyo District Court, seeking the invalidation of the suspension on the grounds that this violated the team's *sports rights* and *right to use public facilities* (Tokyo District Court Judgment, 26 Mar. 1984, Tokyo High Court Judgment, 31 Jan. 1985. Decision Reports (*Hanrei Jiho*), vol. 1146, 62).

24. Masato Dougauchi & Yoshihisa Hayakawa (eds), *An Introduction to Sports Law* 92 (Kyoto: Minerva Shobou Ltd., April 2011).

Part I. Organization of Sport

Chapter 1. Sports Governance

§1. Governmental Institutions and Bodies

44. In Japan, sports policy used to be under the auspices of MEXT for a time. As aforementioned, traditionally in Japan, sports were viewed as *education*, so it is against this backdrop that MEXT formulated the Japanese sports policy. In other words, it is part of Japan's history that *sports* developed as *education.*

45. However, in recent years, ministries other than MEXT have become involved in developing sports policy, including the Ministry of Economy, Trade and Industry (METI) in terms of sports as an industry, and the Ministry of Health, Labour and Welfare (MHLW) in terms of health. On 1 October 2015, a dedicated Japan Sports Agency was established to oversee the formulation and implementation of sports policy.

46. Broadly speaking, the sports world in Japan has been supported by the aforementioned *school*, *corporate* and *professional sports* systems. However, sports in Japan are typically governed by the following organizations:

- JOC (referred to in Japan as the National Olympic Committee).[25]
- JSPO (the umbrella organization for amateur sports).[26]
- The All Japan High School Athletic Federation (the umbrella organization for high school sports).[27]
- The Nippon Junior High School Physical Culture Association (the umbrella organization for junior high school sports).[28]
- Japan Professional Sports Association (this association includes professional sports bodies).
- JTL (this alliance represents the ball-game sports of the corporate sports system).

25. The JOC English website is available at: http://www.joc.or.jp/english/.
26. The JSPO English website is available at: http://www.japan-sports.or.jp/english/index.html.
27. The All Japan High School Athletic Federation Japanese website is available at: http://www.zen-koutairen.com/.
28. The Nippon Junior High School Physical Culture Association Japanese website is available at: http://njpa.sakura.ne.jp.

It should also be noted that the body governing sports for the disabled is the Japan Para-Sports Association (JPSA).[29] The Japan Paralympic Committee (JPC) is part of the JPSA.[30] Under the auspices of the various umbrella sports associations stated above, there are also many separate sports associations as well as regional/ prefectural sports bodies in existence.

47. In Japan, there is no special type of legal entity for sports associations. Thus, they acquire legal personality based on general corporate law (please note, however, in relation to schools, there exists a specific system of legal personality called the *incorporated educational institution*).

§2. National Olympic Committee and Sports Associations

48. Under the umbrella of the JOC and the JSPO, there are various types of sports organizations, most of which possess the legal personality of incorporated non-profit organizations (NPOs), such as incorporated associations, incorporated foundations and specific NPOs. Furthermore, there are many voluntary associations that have not acquired legal personality (e.g., associations for disabled sports).

49. On the whole, professional sports clubs are run as for-profit corporations. However, there are cases such as with the J-League club *Montedio Yamagata* where clubs operated as non-profit corporations (Montedio Yamagata operated as a non-profit until 2014. It currently operates as a for-profit entity).[31] Also, the governing bodies in both professional baseball and football are run as incorporated associations (non-profit corporations). However, recently established leagues (e.g., leagues formed in 2005, including independent baseball leagues) are mainly operated as for-profit corporations. Nonetheless, the operating company of the B.League, which was established in 2015, is a non-profit corporation (the former bj-league was absorbed into this new entity).

50. In December 2008, the reform of the public service corporations in Japan was facilitated. In relation to non-profit corporations, only those that were granted public interest accreditation by the government or regional public institutions were eligible as public interest corporations to preferential tax status under the amended tax system.

51. A major impetus behind this measure was that some bodies which were granted public interest status before the reform were not considered to have had particularly high public interest credentials. Accordingly, up until this reform, there existed many sports associations, both as NPOs and public interest corporations. Many such sports associations faced the stark choice of whether to apply to become

29. The JPSA Japanese website is available at: http://www.jsad.or.jp/.
30. The Japan Paralympics Committee Japanese website is available at: http://www.jsad.or.jp/paralympic/jpc/.
31. The Montedio Yamagata Japanese website is available at: http://www.montedio.or.jp/.

public interest corporations. Otherwise, these bodies were being forced to give up that choice and become regular non-profit corporations. For example, baseball chose to become a regular non-profit corporation, whereas football chose to become a public interest entity.

52. In August 2010 (and even as recent as in March 2011), there were a string of sumo wrestling scandals involving drugs, match-fixing and baseball betting that shook Japan to the core (these scandals are referred to in more detail below in the 'Match-Fixing in Sumo Wrestling' section). In reaction to the scandals, MEXT declared on 26 August 2010 in its report (entitled 'The Strategy for Sports Nation: Sport Community – Nippon') that reforms needed to occur in the governance of sports associations.[32] Article 4 of this MEXT report called for the strengthening of governance in sports associations as well as for greater transparency in their management and administration.

53. The report also said that in order to strengthen sports governance, a special committee of sports association representatives and influential academic experts should be set up. This committee was to be charged with formulating guidelines in relation to the organizational operation of sports associations. These guidelines were then to be used as a basis to improve the overall system of sports associations, through providing financial assistance for national associations, and promoting aid from specific sports funds and the Sports Promotion Lottery.

54. It was against this background in autumn 2010 that MEXT commissioned the 'Sports Governance Committee', set up within the Japan Sports Arbitration Agency (JSAA), to draw up a 'Governance Guidebook' aimed towards sports associations.[33] On top of this, the BSA, newly established in June 2011, places the following duty on sports associations in Article 5(2) which reads 'Sports associations shall, for the purpose of appropriately carrying out work to promote sports, endeavour to ensure transparency in such work as well as establishing standards in relation to the said work activities which the sports associations themselves must strictly observe.' In March 2015, MEXT published the Good Governance Guidelines for National Sport Federation for sporting organizations.[34] And finally, in 2019, Japan Sports Agency has published the 'Governance Code for National Sport Federation Members'[35] by which each sports federation are required to explain its compliance (and subject to compliance audits). Japan Sports Agency has also published 'Governance Code for General Sport Organizations' to encourage sports organizations (other than the federations above) to realize their better governance.

55. Due to the emergence of famous sports stars, the attention on sports associations increases dramatically, which in itself brings a large social responsibility.

32. MEXT, *The Strategy for Sports Nation: Sport Community – Nippon* (MEXT 2010).
33. JSAA, *Governance Guidebook* (JSAA 2011), the guidebook is available in Japanese at: http://www.jsaa.jp/release/pdf/110912.pdf.
34. At http://www.jsaa.jp/ws/goverreport2014_01en.pdf.
35. https://www.mext.go.jp/en/news/topics/detail/1418822.htm.

In fact, when considering the significance of some matters which sports associations decide upon (e.g., selection of representative athletes for major tournaments like the Olympics), it goes without saying that measures should be taken at the national level to strengthen this type of governance.

56. It is obvious that sports associations are independent bodies and their autonomy should be respected. However, it is difficult to say that the operations of sports associations are akin to those of management professionals because it is frequently the case that the power structure of these bodies is based on promotion by seniority, including former players.[36] Moreover, as a high number of sports associations in Japan are managed by people who are not paid, there is a tendency towards irresponsibility by such managers.

57. It is expected that the above Governance Codes will be effectively implemented to address issues such as board selection, information disclosure, guarantees for the transparency of rules, and impartiality in dispute resolution.

36. Masato Dougauchi & Yoshihisa Hayakawa (eds), *An Introduction to Sports Law* 88 (Kyoto: Minerva Shobou Ltd., April 2011).

Chapter 2. Public Regulation

§1. Fundamental Rights

I. Image Rights

58. In Japan, it is frequently the case that players' image rights are managed by the club or sports association to which the player belongs. In contrast, throughout Europe and America, such rights are usually managed by the players (including agent and management companies) and players' associations.

59. Essentially, it is generally thought that image rights derive from the individual's personality, so in basic terms, these rights belong to the player. Nevertheless, in Japan, image rights have been developed gradually through judicial precedent. Also, until comparatively recently revenue from image rights was not so great and the awareness of these rights was lacking among the players. Hence, it was very common for clubs and sports associations to manage the players' image rights.

60. As the sports business developed in Japan, it became increasingly inevitable that revenue from image rights could not be ignored. Alongside this, the players' heightened awareness of these rights led to their wanting more than ever to manage their own images. A significant driving force behind these developments in recent years has been the increase in management companies and agents providing services for players.

61. For instance, in 1977, in order to maximize returns from image usage fees from its sponsors, the JOC implemented the *Gambare Nippon! Campaign* (*Come On Japan! Campaign*) and began managing the image rights of all the athletes belonging to the associations of each Olympic sport.

62. This created a situation where these athletes were completely unable to freely manage their own image rights. However, as the athletes' awareness of their rights burgeoned, it became more difficult for the JOC to maintain its image rights' system. Consequently, in 2005, such athletes acquired the option to manage their own image rights or entrust these to the JOC (entitled the 'Symbol Athlete System').

63. In Japan's two major professional sports, baseball and football, players' image rights are still controlled by the clubs. For instance, on the basis of Article 16 in the Nippon Professional Baseball (NPB) Uniform Player Contract, the NPB clubs have all the rights to commercially use and manage the players' image rights. The

Japan Professional Baseball Players Association (JPBPA) challenge to this inequitable situation led to a legal battle in the courts.[37]

64. A similar situation has also befallen football because according to Article 8(4) of the JFA Player Contract, players must obtain their club's prior written consent to 'exploit and/or license the exploitation of the Player's Image (including use on the internet)'. Based on this provision the clubs effectively manage the players' image rights. As aforementioned, the Japan Pro-Footballers Association (JPFA) is demanding reform to this provision on the grounds of the French for International Federation of Association Football (FIFA) Circular Letter no. 1171.[38]

65. Regarding the national team football players, one must obtain approval from the JFA, rather than the clubs, when using their image rights collectively for merchandising (Article 6 of the JFA Incidental Business Regulations). This provision stipulates that as a general rule, the JFA can *comprehensively use* the image rights of the national team for merchandising purposes without charge when there are *six players or more*. Article 9 of the above Regulations stipulates that the JFA can *comprehensively use* the images of national team players for both JFA newsletters/ reports and advertising activities.

66. In Japan, as a consequence of these circumstances, although players can themselves enter image rights agreements for non-comprehensive usages, in actuality their clubs and sports associations are still largely involved in this process.

II. Image Rights in Baseball

67. For many years in the NPB, the clubs have fully controlled all matters concerned with players' image rights. This is in massive contrast to the MLB where the players' image rights are their own property and are controlled by the players and the Major League Baseball Players Association (MLBPA), accordingly.

68. Since the NPB clubs started controlling and exploiting the players' image rights without individually bargaining with the players and the JPBPA, it has been a continual source of frustration for these parties. For instance, in the 1990s, various problems occurred such as the NPB not distributing image rights usage fees, and also exploiting the images in a manner the players found egregious.

69. In 2000, the NPB granted Konami Corporation (a computer-game publisher) the exclusive right to exploit the players' image rights in the professional baseball computer game. From this, it transpired that other computer-game publishers could

37. Tokyo District Court Judgment, 1 Aug. 2006, Decision Times (*Hanrei Taimuzu*), vol. 1265, 212; first appeal: Tokyo Intellectual Property High Court Judgment, of 25 Feb. 2008; second appeal: Supreme Court of Japan Judgment, 15 Jun. 2010.
38. FIFA Circular no. 1171, *Professional Football Player Contracts Minimum Requirements* (FIFA, 24 Nov. 2008), this is available at: https://digitalhub.fifa.com/m/934c77c17126323/original/fpxmgfy6clfifyrnxteh-pdf.pdf.

not use the players' images in their baseball games without Konami's consent. Please note, that regarding this exclusive agreement, on 22 April 2003, the Japan Fair Trade Commission (JFTC) warned Konami about its conduct in connection with alleged violations of the Anti-Monopoly Act. The NPB also received a caution.[39]

70. As a result of the NPB clubs entering into the exclusive contract with Konami without holding any prior negotiations with the players and JPBPA, these parties have vociferously opposed the manner in which the clubs manage the players' image rights. In November 2000, the JPBPA declared that, like the MLBPA, it was going to manage the players' image rights in relation to computer games. Consequently, this stance led to an escalation of legal action with the NPB clubs.

71. The clubs claimed that the provisions of Article 16 of the NPB Uniform Player's Contract granted the clubs an exclusive licence to commercially exploit the players' images, including for computer games. On the other hand, the JPBPA's view was that Article 16 merely stipulated that the clubs could use the players' images for advertising, such as at matches, and that it did not amount to licence for general commercial use. Furthermore, the JPBPA rebutted the NPB by stating Article 16 was originally modelled on the MLB Uniform Player's Contract, and that in America, it was determined that the right to exploit the image rights commercially belonged to the players.

72. In the end, the players lost their case in a District Court judgment at first instance,[40] and in two further judgments on appeal.[41]

III. Image Rights in Football

73. Even in the J-League, the players' image rights are fully managed and controlled by the clubs (Article 97 of the J-League Regulations and Article 8 of the JFA Standard Players' Contract). The JPFA is actively working towards the liberalization of these image rights for the players.

74. In relation to this point, FIFA and FIFPro (World Players' Union: The Worldwide Representative Organization for All Professional Football Players) agreed upon the provisions of FIFA's Circular no. 1171. This circular was released by FIFA to all member associations on 24 November 2008. The JPFA is using the image rights article (Article 6) stipulated in this circular below, as a basis to push the JFA towards liberalizing the management of the image rights for the players. Article 6 of the FIFA Circular no. 1171 reads:

---

39. JFTC press release: *JFTC Warns Konami Corporation Against Unfair Trade Practices Through Sub-licence Agreements* (JFTC 22 Apr. 2003), the English translation is available at: https://www.jftc.go.jp/en/pressreleases/yearly_2003/apr/individual_000389.html.
40. Tokyo District Court Judgment, 1 Aug. 2006, Decision Times (*Hanrei Taimuzu*), vol. 1265, 212.
41. First appeal: Intellectual Property High Court Judgment, of 25 Feb. 2008. Second appeal: Supreme Court of Japan Judgment, 15 Jun. 2010.

6. Image rights

6.1 The Club and the Player have to agree how the player's image rights are exploited, if applicable.

6.2 As a recommendation and principle, the individual player may exploit his rights by himself (if not conflicting with clubs' sponsors/partners) while the Club may exploit the Players' image rights as part of a group and/or the whole squad.[42]

§2. Governmental Conditions and Permits

I. Issues Concerning the Eligibility of Foreigners to Participate in Sports

A. *Introduction*

75. Irrespective of whether sports are amateur or professional, in Japan, there are various cases where the eligibility of foreigners to participate in such sports is restricted by the rules of sports associations.

76. Foreigners are classified as those people without Japanese citizenship (the requirements for acquiring Japanese citizenship are stipulated in the Nationality Act).[43] In fact, it has been recognized in a Supreme Court judgment that such parties possess the human rights espoused under the Constitution of Japan.[44] However, regarding the extent to which these specific human rights are guaranteed for foreigners, it is generally considered that the substance of the rights should be determined on an individual basis.[45]

B. *Cases in Relation to Amateur Sports*

77. Eligibility to participate in Japan's major amateur sports event, the National Sports Festival, where all forty-seven prefectures nationwide compete against each other, is restricted to people of *Japanese nationality*. In fact, lawsuits have been brought by various foreign athletes claiming that this restriction infringes the Constitution. However, in each lawsuit, the restriction has been judged as *reasonable* and thereby *constitutional*.[46]

---

42. *See* FIFA Circular no. 1171.
43. *Nationality Act*, law no. 147 of 1950 and amendment law no. 88 of 2008.
44. Supreme Court of Japan Judgment, 4 Oct. 1978, Supreme Court of Japan, Civil Decisions Reporter (*Minshu*), vol. 32, nos 7 & 1223.
45. *Ibid.*
46. *See*, for example: Fukui District Court Judgment, 3 Aug. 1993, Decision Times (*Hanrei Taimuzu*), vol. 854, 195; and Supreme Court of Japan Judgment, 11 Jun. 2004.

78. In light of these lawsuits, the JSPO, which hosts the National Sports Festival, extended the eligibility to participate in the festival to people without Japanese nationality who are permanent residents (including many Koreans and Taiwanese who have long resided in Japan) and to foreign students below the age of 18 that met certain criteria. These criteria are that the foreign student in question has to belong to a 'school' as defined under Article 1 of the School Education Act (SEA),[47] as well as being resident in Japan for one year or more at the time of application for the festival.

C. Cases in Relation to Professional Sports

79. In professional sports, foreign player quotas exist, so it is commonplace that the eligibility of foreigners to participate in such sports is restricted. The main cases of such restrictions are covered below.

D. Nippon Professional Baseball

80. In principle, players without Japanese citizenship are considered as *foreign players*, who are restricted by the foreign player quota. However, according to Article 82 of the NPB Agreement, the foreigners shall be treated the same as Japanese citizens if they meet any of the following requirements before concluding a playing contract:

(1) foreigners who have been educated in schools in Japan (including junior high and high schools) for three years or more;
(2) foreigners who have been educated in universities in Japan for four years or more; and
(3) foreigners who have been resident in Japan for five years or more and who have enrolled with Japan Amateur Baseball Association (JABA) amateur teams for three seasons or more.

Please note that there is a special stipulation for foreign players who do not satisfy the three-year or four-year term requirements of (1) or (2) respectively. Basically if such players, after turning professional, have resided in Japan for a total of five years, subject to the NPB Executive Committee's approval, these players will not be counted as part of the foreign quota.

81. Furthermore, the same article also stipulates that when foreign players become free agents following eight seasons being registered in a Japanese professional team's top roster, those players shall also not be restricted by the foreign player quota. The restrictions of the foreign player quota are stated below (Article 82(2) of the NPB Agreement):

47. *School Education Act*, law no. 26 of 1947 and amendment law no. 98.

– There are no restrictions on the number of foreign players a club can contract with.
– In an official game a maximum of four foreign quota registered players can play. However, not all four players can be registered as fielders or pitchers. A maximum combination of 'three pitchers and one fielder' or 'three fielders and one pitcher' can be registered for an official game.

E. *Professional Football*

82. In principle, players without Japanese citizenship are considered as *foreign players,* who are restricted by the foreign player quota. However, according to Article 2-1(9)(1) of the Regulations on Registration and Transfers of Players by the JFA, each team can exclude one player from the foreign quota if this player was born in Japan and satisfies either of the categories listed below:

(1) a person who is completing or has completed their compulsory education as defined under Article 5 of the Basic Education Act at a school defined under Article 1 of the SEA; or
(2) a person who has graduated from a school defined under Article 1 of the SEA or a university.

The restrictions of the foreign player quota in Japan are stated below:

Professional football clubs outside of J-League:

– Each team can only register a maximum of three foreign players. However, by way of exception, teams can also sign contracts with players under twenty who are on 'C' professional contracts (maximum annual salary of JPY 4.6 million – excluding consumption taxes) and amateur players. In principle, a team's foreign quota must not exceed five players.

Professional football clubs in J-League:

– Each team may register an unlimited number of foreign players.
– Up to the following numbers of foreign players may be entered into a game.

Division 1: 5 players
Division 2: 4 players
Division 3: 4 players

– Players from countries with a cooperation relationship with J-League are excluded from the entry quotas above. As of 20 November 2021, J-League has cooperation relationships with Thailand, Vietnam, Myanmar, Cambodia, Singapore, Indonesia, Malaysia, and Qatar.

II. Issues Concerning the Eligibility of Females to Participate in Sports

83. In Japan, there is no American Title IX type of sexual discrimination law. In fact, there are no major examples of legal disputes concerning unreasonable sexual discrimination for the eligibility of females to participate in sport. However, for instance, in sumo wrestling, it is forbidden by long-standing tradition that women enter the sumo ring. The matter as to whether this amounts to unreasonable sexual discrimination has sometimes arisen.

84. Furthermore, it has become evident in the so-called *hierarchical society* of sports that many cases of sexual harassment have occurred towards females when people in authority such as coaches and sports association directors abuse their dominant positions.

85. There has been a case in Japan where a female corporate team badminton player was forcibly raped and sexually assaulted by a male director of a regional Badminton Association. The victim was successful in a lawsuit demanding damages for pain and suffering against the director. Such cases, however, are merely the tip of the iceberg.

§3. Tort Law

I. Legal Responsibility in Sports

86. Typically, legal responsibility arises in a sport when accidents occur. Also, the nature of sports means that there are many accompanying risks in the various accidents that can happen. Broadly speaking, there are three types of legal responsibility that arise from such accidents: (1) civil responsibility; (2) criminal responsibility; and (3) administrative responsibility.

87. First, civil responsibility indicates the liability for damages when the injured party in an accident makes a damages claim against the party at fault. Civil responsibility is usually determined by Articles 709 (Damages in Torts) and 415 (Damages due to Default) of the Civil Code.[48]

88. Article 709 states that a person who has intentionally or negligently infringed any right or legally protected interest of others shall be liable to compensate for any damages resulting in consequence.

89. There are five requirements to establish this tort: (1) the capacity to take responsibility; (2) intention or negligence; (3) illegality; (4) the occurrence of damage; and (5) a causal connection between the party at fault and the damage.

48. *Civil Code,* law no. 89 of 1896 and amendment law no. 78 of 2006.

90. The parties who cause the said damage are usually pursued for legal responsibility. However, it is also often the case that employers are pursued for liability under Article 715 of the Civil Code. In the event that the party at fault is a public officer, according to Article 1 of the State Redress Act (SRA),[49] the state or the regional/prefectural public entity shall assume responsibility to compensate for the resulting damage. When there are contractual relations between a perpetrator and a victim, in addition to Article 709 of the Civil Code, the victim can also seek damages under Article 415 for defaults and failure to perform obligations under the said contract.

91. There are advantages to pursuing legal responsibility under Article 415, as there is a reduced burden of proof (for tortious liability the victim has to prove the perpetrator's intent or neglect, whereas for default liability it is necessary for the perpetrator to prove he/she was not at fault) and a longer damages limitation period.

92. Second, criminal responsibility refers to liability in relation to committing crimes which are subject to punishment through criminal sanctions. There are three requisite elements to a crime: (1) criminal intent; (2) illegality; and (3) culpability.

93. For instance, with boxing as a sport that involves punching an opponent, there is an obvious intent to injure, so element (1) will be fulfilled. However, because boxing is a regulated sport, element (2) will not be fulfilled by virtue of Article 35 of the Penal Code (Justifiable Acts) which states, 'An act performed in accordance with laws and regulations or in the pursuit of lawful business is not punishable.'[50]

94. Consequently, on the whole, there are very few cases of criminal liability in sports. Nevertheless, criminal responsibility can arise in cases where coaches or instructors administer physical punishment or sexually harass athletes and sports players.

95. Finally, administrative responsibility refers to liability where the party at fault is a public officer that can be subject to disciplinary action such as dismissal or a reduction in salary.

96. Below, there is an examination of the tortious liability of the following parties in sports: competitors, instructors, coaches, administrators and facility managers. After this, there is an analysis of issues such as the validity of waiver forms and comparative negligence.

---

49. *State Redress Act*, law no. 125 of 1947.
50. *Penal Code*, law no. 45 of 1907 and amendment law no. 54 of 2007.

II. Sports Competitors and Tort Law

A. Liability and Negligence of Competitors in Sports Accidents

97. Negligence is the breach of a duty of care. A duty of care includes both the obligation to anticipate or foresee the consequences of a given situation and the obligation to avoid these consequences. In the case of sports accidents, determining whether the relevant duty of care has been discharged depends on a comprehensive assessment of the circumstances, such as the competitor's individual attributes (e.g., is the athlete a beginner or advanced, an adult or juvenile, a professional or amateur?), the degree of risk inherent in the sport, and the way in which the accident occurred.[51]

98. In relation to this point, the Tokyo District Court has considered the situation in golf where a golfer on the sixth hole with his/her shot hits and injures another golfer on the fifth hole tee. Basically, the sixth hole golfer will not be at fault if the fifth hole tee was not visible and it is not foreseeable that the ball would land there. On the other hand, it is recognized that the golf course operator would be at fault if there were no protective barriers set up, such as guard nets.[52]

B. Liability and Illegality of Competitors in Sports Accidents

99. Based on the tacit acceptance that risks are inherent in sports, it thereby follows that such risks are not illegal as these are *assumed* by the participants in the sports. In fact, there is a Tokyo District Court judgment concerning an injury during volleyball practice suffered by a player to her right knee when she collided with an opponent who was jumping. The court observed:

> The injury in question does not obviously breach sporting rules and it is ordinarily foreseeable. In fact, when the injury is attributable to actions permitted within that sport, it is appropriate that all participants accept the inherent risks accordingly. Thus, this precludes the wrongfulness/illegality of the act by the athlete who caused the said injury.[53]

100. Furthermore, in another judgment, the Tokyo District Court (*Takushoku University Takuninkai Incident*) recognized that there were four requirements for sporting acts to preclude wrongdoing/illegality:

---

51. Masato Dougauchi & Yoshihisa Hayakawa (eds), *An Introduction to Sports Law* 227 (Kyoto: Minerva Shobou Ltd., April 2011).
52. Tokyo District Court Judgment, 29 May 1985, Decision Reports (*Hanrei Jiho*), vol. 1206, 49.
53. Tokyo District Court Judgment, 27 Feb. 1970, Decision Reports (*Hanrei Jiho*), vol. 594, 454 (author's translation from Japanese).

(1) that the main purpose of the sport in question is for training or discipline which is socially acceptable when considering the nature of the sport in question;
(2) that participants, play in a socially acceptable manner which matches the power and skill of their opponents, as well as observing the sport's rules;
(3) that the extent of the injury to the opponent is socially acceptable; and
(4) that the valid approval of the opponent is acquired.[54]

C. *Liability and Capacity to Assume Liability of Competitors in Sports Accidents*

101. The capacity to assume legal liability is governed by Articles 712 and 713 of the Civil Code, which state that parties should have sufficient intellectual capacity to appreciate the liability for their acts. Thus, if someone has an intellectual capacity of a twelve-year-old child, he or she should be judged as such. For instance, minors that lack sufficient capacity to appreciate the consequences of their actions shall not be liable to compensate for these acts in sports.

102. In such cases, however, the victims of sporting accidents frequently pursue legal responsibility from the people who are obliged to supervise the person without capacity, such as the parents of a minor who caused the accident (Article 714 of the Civil Code). A recent case decided by the Japanese Supreme Court on 9 April 2015 provides a good example. An eleven-year-old boy kicked a football in the school yard after class. The ball landed on a road outside of the field. A passer-by on a motorcycle could not avoid the ball in time and as a result, was killed from falling off the motorcycle. The Court did not find negligence of guardian obligations because 'guardians only have a general duty to instruct and supervise. When a child not under direct supervision of a guardian carries out a conduct that cannot be foreseen as being unsafe to other humans under normal circumstances, the guardians cannot be deemed negligent if the child's conduct happens to cause actual harm to other humans'.[55]

III. Sports Coaches and Instructors and Tort Law

103. It is frequently the case that sports coaches and instructors are held legally liable for sports accidents, such as teachers being responsible for sporting accidents in schools. These school coaches and instructors often not only face personal liability for damages in tort (Article 709 of the Civil Code) but the school can also bear liability in its capacity as an employer (Article 715). A head teacher who supervises the sports coaches and instructors can also be held responsible for the acts of these parties (Article 715(2)). Please note that based on Article 1 of the SRA, the state or

54. Tokyo District Court Judgment, 7 Mar. 1972 (author's translation from Japanese). At http://www.courts.go.jp/app/files/hanrei_jp/032/085032_hanrei.pdf.
55. At http://www.courts.go.jp/app/files/hanrei_jp/032/085032_hanrei.pdf.

the relevant regional/prefectural public body can also be liable for damages caused by the acts of a public high school instructor.

104. Furthermore, schools or educational institutions may not only be liable under tort for sporting accidents but could also be responsible for breaching the safety obligation provisions contained in education agreements between the school and the students.

105. In such cases, just like the aforesaid determination concerning whether the competitor's duty of care has been discharged, when assessing the relevant instructor's negligence (breach of duty of care) or their breach of safety obligation provisions therein, it is necessary to consider the instructor's individual attributes (e.g., Is the athlete a beginner or advanced, an adult or juvenile, a professional or amateur?), the degree of risk inherent in the sport, and the circumstances concerning how the accident occurred.

106. In general, the lower the student's capacity is to appreciate his/her own situation (e.g., elementary school student) the more likely courts will find a breach of the instructor's duty of care and the relevant safety obligation provisions.[56]

IV. Sport Facility Managers and Administrators and Tort

107. There are often cases where facility managers and administrators are pursued for legal responsibility under Article 717 of the Civil Code for sports accidents which occurred due to defective equipment or facilities. Where the accident happens because of defects in publicly managed facilities, the State or relevant regional/prefectural public body is liable in damages (Article 2 or the SRA).

108. Defective is interpreted as meaning a situation where such facilities, which require a certain level of maintenance, are completely lacking in safety. Generally, there are many cases brought against schools in relation to liability for swimming pool accidents, with it often being recognized that these facilities were defective.[57]

109. In determining the existence of *defects*, it is necessary to consider the risks in relation to the potential users and the way in which the sports facility is to be used. On top of this, consideration is also given as to whether guidelines for such facilities have been formulated by sports associations and if there are relevant people management systems in operation.[58]

---

56. Masaru Ogasawara (ed.), et al., *An Introductory Dialogue to Sports Jurisprudence* 281 (2nd edn., Tokyo: Fumashoubo Ltd., April 2007).
57. Please *see* for example, the Fukuoka District Court Judgment, 27 Dec. 1988, Decision Reports (*Hanrei Jiho*), vol. 1310, 124.
58. Masato Dougauchi & Yoshihisa Hayakawa (eds), *An Introduction to Sports Law* 244 (Kyoto: Minerva Shobou Ltd., April 2011).

110. There is a case where a spectator who was injured by a foul ball at a professional baseball game brought a claim against the baseball team, the company that operated the stadium, and the municipality that owned the stadium for damages caused by the *defects* in accordance with Article 717(1) of the Civil Code and Article 2(1) of the SRA. The Supreme Court of Japan ruled on 20 May 2016 that although the plaintiff did not have a claim against the operator and owner of the stadium, he did have a valid claim against the team.

111. Furthermore, there are cases where it has been determined that asphalt grounds for school athletics facilities lack safety. However, due to the reason that such accidents cannot be avoided, even assuming that these grounds are soil-based, it is not acknowledged that there is a causal connection between the ground *defects* and the corresponding accidents.[59]

V. Validity of Waiver Forms

112. Sports competitors are frequently made to sign waiver forms that completely discard their right to seek damages and the right to defend themselves in criminal cases. In Japan, there have been a number of legal judgments which have rejected the validity of such waiver forms. For instance, in one case the Tokyo District Court ruled that this kind of waiver form was void as an act against public policy under Article 90 of the Civil Code.[60]

113. Furthermore, according to Article 8 of the Consumer Contracts Act, such waiver forms will be void as consumer contract clauses, if they seek to totally exclude a business operator from liability to compensate damages to a consumer when these arise from the business operator's default.[61]

VI. Damages and Partial Negligence

114. If the liability of a party is recognized in tort or default of contractual performance, that party will be responsible to bear the resulting damages. In principle, the amount of these damages shall be determined with reference to monetary value (Articles 722(1) and 417 of the Civil Code). However, in the event the victim is also negligent, the court shall take this into account to potentially reduce the amount of damages payable to that party (Articles 722(2) and 418 of the Civil Code).

59. Tokyo District Court Judgment 18 Sep. 1978, Decision Reports (*Hanrei Jiho*), vol. 911, 115.
60. Tokyo District Court Judgment 20 Jun. 2001, Decision Times (*Hanrei Taimuzu*), vol. 1074, 219.
61. *Consumer Contracts Act*, law no. 61 of 2000 and amendment law no. 56 of 2006.

VII. Insurance Systems

115. If a party liable in tort or in default of contractual performance has little or no financial standing, the victim shall be without a remedy. Therefore, it is common practice that competitors in sports join injury and public liability insurance schemes. As a consequence, in Japan, there have been various insurance schemes which have come onto the market, including:

- *Mutual Aid Disaster Insurance* provides compensation to students who are under the supervision of schools when disasters occur.
- *Sports Safety Insurance* provided by the Japan Sports Safety Association.
- *Official Sports Insurance for Coaches* provided by JSPO.
- Specialist insurance for individual sports such as golf and skiing provided by private insurers.

VIII. Other Cases of Tortious Liability in Relation to Sport

116. There are also damages compensation issues that arise based on the Product Liability Act in relation to defects in sporting equipment.[62] There have also been instances where liability in tort has arisen when mass media violate athletes' privacy rights. This is illustrated in particular by a judgment of the Tokyo District Court which affirmed that the privacy rights of the footballer Hidetoshi Nakata had been breached by the media.[63]

IX. Illegal Gambling and Match-Fixing

117. In Japan, gambling and lotteries are criminal offences.[64] Accordingly, apart from public gambling (horse racing, bicycle racing (keirin), motorbike racing, and boat racing) which is recognized by special laws, and 'toto' the sports lottery game for football matches, sports betting is illegal.[65]

118. Furthermore, there has been a concerted effort in each sport in Japan to prohibit match-fixing following various unsavoury incidents that plagued sports. The first example of this was match-fixing in professional baseball in the so-called *Black Mist Scandal* that occurred from 1969 to 1971, and within which the Japanese *yakuza* (an organized crime syndicate) was heavily involved. Another incident at around the same time concerned large *yakuza* involvement in the fixing of results in the public gambling sports of horse and motorbike racing.

---

62. *Product Liability Act*, law no. 85 of 1994.
63. Tokyo District Court Judgment, 25 Dec. 2000, Decision Reports (*Hanrei Jiho*), vol. 1743, 130.
64. Article 185 of the *Penal Code*.
65. The 'toto' website is available in Japanese at: http://www.toto-dream.com/.

119. Since 1971, Japan remained relatively free of large match-fixing scandals for forty years, until the widespread manipulation of results in sumo wrestling was discovered in early 2011 to once again shock Japanese society to the core. Barring natural disasters and war, this scandal brought about for the first time in history the cancellation of a sumo tournament in March 2011. Together with this, a large number of wrestlers were subject to strict disciplinary actions.

120. This sumo match-fixing scandal was caused by the *mutual cooperation* between sumo wrestlers rather than the *yakuza*-style organized criminal betting, which occurred throughout the aforesaid *Black Mist Scandal.* For instance, match-fixing was used to maintain the excellent records that are expected of the *Yokozuna* and *Ozeki* division sumo wrestlers, and thus protect their status in the sport. In 2015 and 2016, there was much media coverage on the suspension of professional baseball and badminton players for illegal gambling.

121. Below, there are examinations of: the 'Legal System Governing Betting and Lotteries in Japan'; the 'Special Laws Governing Public Gambling'; 'Football Betting as a Means of Sports Promotion'; and 'Match-Fixing in Japan'.

A. *Legal System Governing Betting and Lotteries in Japan*

122. As aforementioned, gambling and lotteries are criminal offences in Japan.

123. Gambling, that is to say, the wagering of one's assets, relies on the result of extrinsic circumstances.[66] Furthermore, the actual act of gambling is, in essence, putting other peoples' assets at risk. These ideas pose a threat to the custom on which the prosperous Japanese economy is based, namely that of working hard to maintain a good livelihood. The criminal law system in Japan recognizes these concepts and that incidental to gambling comes the risk of corruption and theft in society. Therefore, strict regulations have been laid out to prevent and defend against such criminal activity.[67]

124. Private gambling and lotteries in Japan are prohibited by Chapter 23 of the Penal Code. More. Specifically, Article 185 covers gambling; Article 186 covers habitual gambling, the creation of gambling groups, and colluding to profit from gambling and gambling locations; and Article 187 covers the sale of lottery tickets. These articles are set out below.

Article 185 states:

---

66. Masahide Maeda (eds) et al., *Commentaries to the Penal Code* 487 (2nd ed., Koubundo Publishers Inc., 2007).

67. *Ibid.*

> A person who gambles shall be punished by a fine of not more than JPY 500,000 or a petty fine; provided, however, that the same shall not apply to a person who bets a thing which is provided for momentary entertainment.
>
> However, this law is not only limited to people who gamble things for pleasure, it also regulates situations where two or more people together try to profit from a betting game. This law covers all types of items which are gambled (please note, however, that items such as food, drink and tobacco, which are wagered for insignificant amounts are not criminalized under the Penal Code).

Article 186 states:

1. A person who habitually gambles shall be punished by imprisonment with work for not more than three years.
2. A person who, for the purpose of profit, runs a place for gambling or organizes a group of habitual gamblers shall be punished by imprisonment with work for not less than three months but not more than five years.

Paragraph (1) covers the gambling situations stipulated in Article 185, but those of a more serious nature. Paragraph (2) covers situations where people open gambling houses or become so-called *bookies.*

Article 187 states:

1. A person who sells a lottery ticket shall be punished by imprisonment with work for not more than two years or a fine of not more than JPY 1,500,000.
2. A person who acts as an intermediary in the sale of a lottery ticket shall be punished by imprisonment with work for not more than one year or a fine of not more than JPY 1,000,000.
3. Except for the cases provided for in the preceding two paragraphs, a person who delivers or receives a lottery ticket shall be punished by a fine of not more than JPY 200,000 or a petty fine.

Paragraph (1) aims to prevent situations where people sell lottery tickets. Paragraph (2) aims to prevent cases where people, although not selling or purchasing tickets directly, act as brokers in the illicit trading of tickets. Paragraph (3) covers situations where people illicitly transfer or assign lottery tickets.

125. Furthermore, the crime of fraud (Article 246 of the Penal Code) is subject to a maximum of ten years in prison and can be applied to match-fixing.[68]

68. *See* Masahide Maeda (eds) et al., *Commentaries to the Penal Code* (2nd ed., Koubundo Publishers Inc., 2007) *See also*, Supreme Court of Japan Judgment, 8 May 1951, 5 Crim. Cases, no. 6, 1004.

B. Special Laws Governing Public Gambling

126. As discussed above, in Japan, every private act of gambling or sale of lottery tickets is strictly prohibited by criminal law. However, after the Second World War, public gambling was allowed, under the auspices of the Japanese government and is recognized by special laws for the promotion of regional economies, industry and manufacturing.[69] The different types of public gambling are as follows: horse racing, bicycle racing (keirin), motorbike racing and motorboat racing.

1. Horse Racing

127. The law governing horse racing in Japan is the Horse Racing Act (HRA).[70] As stipulated in the HRA, the institutions charged with controlling horse racing matters are the Japan Racing Association for national horse racing and the prefectural governments of Japan (prefectural governments) for regional horse racing (Article 1 of the HRA). Under the HRA, the main penal rules for match-fixing are listed below.

Article 31 states:

> An imprisonment at forced labour of three years or less, or a fine of JPY 3,000,000 or less, shall be imposed on a person falling under one of the following Items:
>
> 1. A person who administers a drug or medicine which temporarily stimulates or depresses the racing performance of a horse declared to start.
> 2. A jockey who prevents a horse from displaying its full capabilities in a race to gain financial profits for himself/herself or for others.

Article 32-2 states:

> An imprisonment at forced labour of three years or less shall be imposed on a trainer, jockey, or a person who assists with the feed and care, or training of racehorses in the event he/she receives, demands, or promises a bribe in connection with a race. An imprisonment at forced labour of five years or less shall be imposed in the event a dishonest act or omission has been committed as a result of these acts.

69. Masaru Ogasawara (ed.), et al., *An Introductory Dialogue to Sports Jurisprudence* 52 (2nd edn., Tokyo: Fumashoubo Ltd., April 2007).
70. *Horse Racing Act*, law no. 158 of 1948.

2. Bicycle Racing (Keirin)

128. The law governing keirin in Japan is the Keirin Act.[71] As stipulated in the Keirin Act, the institutions charged with controlling keirin matters are the prefectural governments and municipalities decided by the Home Affairs Minister. The keirin regulatory authority is METI (Article 50 of the Keirin Act). However, METI has granted the Japan Keirin Association (an incorporated foundation) responsibility for ensuring that keirin meetings are properly regulated. Under the Keirin Act, the main penal rule for match-fixing is listed below.

Article 60 states:

> An imprisonment at forced labour of three years or less shall be imposed on a keirin rider in the event he/she receives, demands, or promises a bribe in connection with a race. An imprisonment at forced labour of five years or less shall be imposed in the event a dishonest act or omission has been committed as a result of these acts.

3. Motorbike Racing

129. The law governing motorbike racing in Japan is the Motorbike Racing Act (MRA).[72] In motorbike racing law, the Japanese parliament is responsible for deciding, by resolution, the authorities charged with administering motorbike racing matters. These institutions are: the prefectural governments; Osaka City; Kyoto City; Yokohama City; Nagoya City; Kobe City; each of the wards of Tokyo Metropolis where a relevant association is established; and municipalities where a motorbike racing track is currently in existence (Article 3(1) of the MRA). The main penal rule for match-fixing in the MRA is listed below.

Article 65 states:

> An imprisonment at forced labour of three years or less shall be imposed on a motorbike rider in the event he/she receives, demands, or promises a bribe in connection with a race. An imprisonment at forced labour of five years or less shall be imposed in the event a dishonest act or omission has been committed as a result of these acts.

71. *Keirin Act*, law no. 209 of 1948.
72. *Motorbike Racing Act*, law no. 208 of 1950.

4. Motorboat Racing

130. The law governing motorboat racing in Japan is the Motorboat Racing Act (MboatRA).[73] In motorboat racing law, the Japanese parliament is responsible for deciding, by resolution, the authorities charged with administering motorboat racing matters. To this end, the Home Affairs Minister should take account of the special economic and political circumstances of each particular municipality or administrative division (Article 2(1) of the MboatRA). Under the MboatRA, the main penal rule for match-fixing is listed below.

Article 72 states:

> An imprisonment at forced labour of three years or less shall be imposed on a motorboat racer in the event he/she receives, demands, or promises a bribe in connection with a race. An imprisonment at forced labour of five years or less shall be imposed in the event a dishonest act or omission has been committed as a result of these acts.

X. Football Betting as a Means of Promoting the Sport

131. The law governing football betting is the Sports Promotion Lottery Act (SPLA).[74] As stipulated by the SPLA, MEXT is the regulatory authority for football betting. Furthermore, the main objectives of MEXT under the SPLA are to ensure that necessary funds are raised for sports promotion and to confirm that any initiative it sets up is effectively administered.

132. So far, football is the only sport to be utilized for sports promotion betting initiatives under the SPLA. To this end, the J-League (Article 24(1) of the SPLA) was set up to run various football competitions. These comprise the J-League, the J-League Cup, and the Emperor's Cup. Further, an October 2013 amendment to the SPLA (Article 5(2)) included certain other football competitions, such as Bundesliga, Premier League and FIFA matches (e.g., World Cup) in the toto lottery. However, please note that other football competitions are excluded from the aforementioned initiatives, including the amateur Japan Football League, local leagues, and other foreign football leagues. Moreover, there have also been discussions about including professional baseball, rugby and basketball games in the toto lottery since 2015 but only basketball has been included by a December 2020 amendment to the SPLA. Therefore, basketball betting under the amended SPLA is expected to be introduced as early as 2022.

73. *Motorboat Racing Act*, law no. 242 of 1951.
74. *Sports Promotion Lottery Act*, law no. 63 of 1998.

133. The sole authority charged with administering sports promotion through betting under the SPLA is the Japan Sport Council (JSC) (Article 3 of the SPLA).[75] By order of MEXT, JSC will select certain J-League games (Designated Games) on which betting can take place. After the games, any gambler in possession of a winning ticket, in line with the rules stipulated by MEXT, will receive a payout of their relevant winnings (Article 2 of the SPLA).

134. Football betting tickets can be purchased either online, at convenience stores or from specially licensed betting shops. However, as stipulated by Articles 9 and 10 of the SPLA, the following parties cannot purchase or receive transfers of football betting tickets: people under nineteen; government officials working to promote other sports; JSC staff; J-League members of staff; and all the J-League club employees, representatives, directors, players, coaches, J-League match referees and commissioners. Criminal sanctions such as imprisonment or fines (Articles 32 and 42 of the SPLA) can be imposed on any of the above-mentioned parties in breach of the SPLA.

135. Under the SPLA, the main penal rules for match-fixing are listed below.

Article 37 states:

> An imprisonment at forced labour of three years or less shall be imposed on a J-League official, employee and/or any parties stipulated in Article 10(4)–(6) in the event he/she receives, demands, or promises a bribe in the course of his/her duties and/or involvement relating to the Designated Games as prescribed in Article 24. An imprisonment at forced labour of five years or less shall be imposed in the event a dishonest act or omission has been committed as a result of these acts.

Article 42 states:

> In a Designated Game, an imprisonment at forced labour of two years or less, or a fine of JPY 1,000,000 or less shall be imposed on a person who has conspired to conduct a game in a manner damaging to fair and impartial football games.

75. The JSC website in Japanese available at: https://www.jpnsport.go.jp/.

XI. Match-Fixing in Japan

A. *Black Mist Scandal in Professional Baseball*

136. The *Black Mist Scandal* that rocked professional baseball occurred between 1969 and 1971. This scandal involved several players belonging to the then *Nishitetsu Lions* (now the team is called the *Saitama Seibu Lions*) taking bribes from members of the *yakuza* to throw games. As a result of these actions, the NPB commissioners handed down league sanctions to the players involved, which ranged from one-year to lifetime bans.

137. As a consequence of the *Black Mist Scandal*, the NPB introduced new regulations to the NPB Agreement to prohibit cheating and dishonest conduct, such as trying to throw games. Article 177 of the NPB Agreement prohibits the conduct listed below, and in the event that any of these provisions are violated, the NPB commissioners are authorized to impose lifetime bans.

Article 177:

1. Acts and/or conduct in any NPB games, designed to fix or influence the outcome of those games, such as: intentionally losing games; attempting to lose games; or neglecting to make best efforts to win games.
2. Acts of collusion by any other parties designed to fix or influence the outcome of games, as stipulated in (1).
3. For the purpose of winning games, providing and/or attempting to provide money and/or goods as compensation to the players, managers, and coaches of other teams, in order for such parties to play a role or be deemed to play a role in winning games for their team.
4. Extorting or receiving money and/or goods as compensation for having played a role or being deemed to have played a role in winning a game.
5. Providing or attempting to provide money and/or goods as compensation to referees and/or judges for the purpose of such parties to influence or be deemed to influence the outcome of a game through their acts.
6. An NPB team betting on games with which the team is directly involved.

138. Furthermore, Article 180 of the NPB Agreement prohibits the conduct listed below, and in the event that any of these provisions are violated, the NPB commissioners are authorized to impose one-year or indefinite bans.

Article 180:

1. Associating with and/or acting in concert with habitual baseball gamblers and Anti-Social Forces (organized crime groups and their members, corporate racketeers, and groups that have the potential for violence or social unrest); being entertained, receiving money and/or goods; or in any other manner receiving, providing, demanding, proposing, or promising profits from or to such gamblers.

2. An NPB team betting on games with which the team is not directly involved.

139. Due to regulations like these, ever since the *Black Mist Scandal*, each professional baseball team has paid much attention to the off-field associations their players keep. As a result, links between the players and the *yakuza* have gradually diminished.

B. Match-Fixing in Motorbike Racing and Horse Racing

140. It was further discovered that some baseball players connected with the above *Black Mist Scandal* were also involved in match-fixing within motorbike racing. Many motorbike racers were arrested in relation to this match-fixing scandal.

141. Furthermore, four years prior to the *Black Mist Scandal* in 1965, match-fixing in horse racing was widespread in an incident called the *Yamaoka Scandal*. This scandal led to the arrest of three national horse racing jockeys and two *yakuza* members. The three arrested jockeys and another jockey who was not arrested but participated in the scandal were sanctioned with lifetime bans by the horse racing authorities.

142. Following the *Yamaoka Scandal*, the horse racing authorities consolidated their regulations through measures such as restricting access to stables and preserving the race post times of jockeys and horses (e.g., restricting the contact with outsiders).

C. Match-Fixing in Sumo Wrestling

143. The discovery in early 2011 of the match-fixing scandal embroiling the world of sumo wrestling sent shockwaves and massive consternation through Japanese society. This scandal and the method of match-fixing were uncovered by an investigation into a large-scale 2010 baseball betting problem among the sumo wrestlers. In relation to the 2010 problem, it came to light that various parties related to sumo, including dozens of current wrestlers, participated in this illegal baseball betting. The punishment handed out for this by the Japan Sumo Association (JSA) involved the stable master *Otake* and *Ozeki Kotomitsuki* being expelled, along with the suspension of many other wrestlers.[76]

76. The JSA website in English is available at: http://www.sumo.or.jp/eng/. At http://www.badminton.or.jp/news/2016/20160410.pdf; http://www.badminton.or.jp/news/2016/20160419.pdf.

144. In essence, match-fixing in sumo wrestling is used by wrestlers for the purpose of maintaining their status in the sport, through the trading of results by throwing or fixing bouts for money. The overriding aim of this conduct is for wrestlers to protect their own positions and not to carry out illegal betting.

145. In the 2011 scandal, it was discovered that through mobile phone text messages, some wrestlers had gone as far as agreeing which winning moves would be used during bouts and how the losing opponent should fall. This type of intent to fix bouts, unlike with the aforementioned laws on public gambling (such as the HRA), is not regulated by the law. However, the JSA has seen a problem with this conduct as it infringes its own internal regulations concerning the wrestlers' duty to always perform to their maximum level.

146. The match-fixing scandal forced the JSA to cancel the 2011 spring tournament and led to many wrestlers being advised to retire or hit with suspensions. It is said that the factors behind this match-fixing scandal include the massive economic disparity between the *Juryo* and *Makushita* divisions and the controversial 2003 abolition of the Public Injury System. The latter system used to allow a wrestler who had been injured in the ring during an official tournament to keep their rank in the subsequent tournaments.

D. Illegal Betting in Professional Baseball

147. In October 2015, three professional baseball players of Yomiuri Giants were found guilty of betting on baseball. NPB imposed permanent suspension on the three players in accordance with Article 180 of the Professional Baseball Agreement. The team terminated its contracts with the players. One of the three players was arrested the following year for aiding and abetting illegal wagering and gambling.

148. Furthermore, another Yomiuri Giants player was found to have engaged in betting on baseball. NPB imposed a one-year suspension pursuant to Article 180 of the Professional Baseball Agreement, and the team terminated its contract with the player.

149. In response to these events, the twelve teams of NPB and the JPBPA issued statements aiming at the prevention of similar conduct. To encourage self-initiated remedial measures and prevent future offences, NPB also announced that it would allow players who came clean between 6 and 25 of April 2016 to reduce their suspension to one year. Nonetheless, no one reported himself.

E. Illegal Betting in Badminton

150. In April 2016, a group of nine badminton players, including former and current national team players, were found to have been gambling illegally in casinos.

In response, the Japan Badminton Association imposed different sanctions on the players depending on the seriousness of their violations, including deregistration, cancellation of the privilege to represent the national team, six-month suspension, suspension for an indefinite period and a severe warning.

§4. TAX

151. There are various forms of sports clubs. In general, professional teams are registered as business corporations (stock companies) which are obliged to pay corporation tax. In relation to corporations in the public interest, NPOs or associations or foundations without juridical personality, such bodies shall be liable only to pay corporation tax when they conduct profit-making business activities (Article 4(1) of the Corporation Tax Act and Article 70(1) of the Act to Promote Specified Non-Profit Activities).[77, 78]

152. On top of the obligation to pay corporation tax, the above corporations are also liable to corporation inhabitant taxes (including prefectural and city inhabitant taxes) as well as business enterprise taxes. For corporations with an annual taxable sales income exceeding JPY 10 million, these will also be subject to the consumption tax.

153. Athletes' employment-related taxation is discussed in Part II below.

§5. SPORTS JUSTICE

I. Legal Basis for Justice in Sports

154. Article 2(5) of the BSA (The Promotion of Sports for Disabled People) provides that no participants in sports should be subjected to *unjust discriminatory treatment*. Article 2(8) lays out the provision that all sports activities should be *fairly and appropriately administered.*

155. In relation to the obligations of the sports associations, Article 2(2) stipulates that the main purpose of the work of these associations is for the promotion of sports. In light of this, there are two regulations below which are particularly pertinent.

Article 5(2):

> Sports associations shall, for the purpose of appropriately carrying out work to promote sports, endeavour to ensure transparency in such work as well as

---

77. *Corporation Tax Act*, law no. 34 of 1965 and amendment law no. 65 of 2010.
78. *Act to Promote Specified Non-Profit Activities*, law no. 7 of 2008 and amendment law no. 28 of 2008.

establishing standards in relation to the said work activities which the sports associations themselves must strictly observe.

Article 5(3):

Sports associations shall endeavour to achieve swift and appropriate resolution to all disputes involving sports.

156. Article 5(2) has been dubbed the *Sports Association Governance* article. As outlined in paragraph 52 above, MEXT in reaction to the scandals embroiling sumo wrestling, declared in its 26 August 2010 report on national sports strategy that reforms needed to occur in the governance of sports associations.

157. Article 4 of this MEXT report called for the strengthening of governance in sports associations as well as for greater transparency in their management and administration. These provisions are now recognized in Article 5(2) of the BSA.

158. Article 5(3) of the BSA places a duty on sports associations to strive for swift and appropriate resolution of disputes involving sports. As shall be outlined in the 'Dispute Settlements' chapter below, when sports disputes occurred in Japan originally there were very few dispute settlement bodies within the sports associations to deal with these. In fact, even where such bodies existed, they were in no way impartial as the adjudicators were frequently unilaterally selected by the sports associations.

159. Furthermore, even despite the establishment of the impartial JSAA in 2003, there are still many sports which are reluctant to use this body. Thus, there remain a high number of sports associations that lack awareness of the concept of *swift and appropriate* dispute resolution. In relation to this, Article 4 of the above MEXT report stipulates:

> It is required of sports associations that they demand the swift and smooth resolution of sports disputes. In order to promote development in effective dispute resolution systems it is necessary to enhance the understanding of associations and athletes in dispute resolution procedures, and also to cultivate the skills of arbitrators and mediators. On top of this, we support the strengthening of the functions of the Japan Sports Arbitration Agency.

160. Article 15 of the BSA stipulates the State's duties in relation to swift and appropriate sports dispute resolution:

> The State shall take necessary measures for guaranteeing the neutrality and impartiality of arbitrations and mediations for sports disputes as well as any measures that contribute to the swift and appropriate resolution of such disputes; and shall guarantee the rights and interests of participants in sports,

through taking measures such as supporting arbitrations and mediations in sports disputes, enhancing the quality of arbitrators and mediators, and increasing understanding of dispute resolution procedures for sports associations.

161. Therefore, as a consequence of Articles 5(3) and 15 of the BSA, it is widely expected that the sports associations will further develop their dispute resolution bodies, which will lead to swifter and more appropriate settlement of disputes. Actually, the newly published 'Governance Code for National Sport Federation Members' (*see* paragraph 54) requires national sports federations to use JSAA as a dispute resolution body.

II. Sports Disputes and the Necessity for Alternative Dispute Resolution

162. In Japan, sports disputes take various forms. Due to the *partial society* nature of the sports world, however, there is a tendency to resolve disputes internally within the relevant sports associations. It is rare that disputes are brought to external judicial bodies such as the courts.[79]

163. On the other hand, this does not mean that the dispute resolution bodies within sports associations in Japan are well developed and reliable. Originally, these bodies themselves did not exist within such organizations, and even where they did these were often highly unfair structures with the adjudicator (the person with the role of judge) being elected by only one side in the dispute. For instance, there are major concerns over the impartiality of adjudicators in professional baseball and the J-League, as these parties are selected by those on the side of the clubs.

164. Although there have been no specific judicial precedents in relation to sports, it has been judged that where the authority to elect adjudicators is inequitably defined (e.g., where only one side in a dispute can elect the mediator), this will be void under Article 90 of the Civil Code as an act against public policy.[80]

165. Accordingly, in order to ensure equitable settlements to sports disputes, the existence of an external dispute resolution body is an absolute necessity. However, it is difficult to depend entirely on the courts as external sports dispute resolution bodies. The reasons for this are provided below.

166. First, resolution in the court system can take a long time and be expensive, so courts are restricted here in their suitability for dealing with sports disputes.

79. Masato Dougauchi & Yoshihisa Hayakawa (eds), *An Introduction to Sports Law* 92 (Kyoto: Minerva Shobou Ltd., April 2011).
80. Please refer to: Osaka District Court Judgment, 2 Feb. 1989, Decision Times (*Hanrei Taimuzu*), vol. 717, 222; and Supreme Court of Japan Judgment, 6 Sep. 1984 Civil Decisions Reporter (*Minshu*), vol. 142, 293.

167. Second, there are some sports disputes which by their nature are not amenable to legal resolution in ordinary courts. According to Article 3(1) of the Court Act,[81] courts are only supposed to handle 'legal disputes'. Here, 'legal disputes' are interpreted by the Supreme Court as such:

> When there is a dispute concerning the existence or not of specific legal rights and obligations, and, which can be permanently resolved through the application of law.[82]

168. Correspondingly, the courts cannot be the forum by which to resolve disputes concerned with decisions in sports and related competition qualification/selection issues. In relation to this point, the Tokyo District Court has struck down a case from a party which demanded the revocation of a penalty imposed by a car racing association for breaching race track rules, because the case was not recognized as a 'legal dispute'.[83]

169. By the same token, various other cases have been decided by the courts on the basis that sports disputes are not 'legal disputes'. For instance, there was a case where a dancer contested a three-year membership suspension imposed by the Eastern Japan Division of the Japan Ballroom Dance Federation.[84] In another case, a golfer challenged the decision of the Japan Senior Golfers' Association to enrol members into a certain class of membership.[85]

170. On the other hand, there have been some sports dispute cases that have been decided by the courts on the premise that these are 'legal disputes'. For instance, there was a case where a boxer's registration was revoked for his lack of amateur status and subsequently banned from competing in various tournaments for one year.[86]

171. In a further case, there were continuous challenges by judokas of the All Japan University Judo Federation against alleged unjust qualification limits imposed by the All Japan Judo Federation. The judokas in question could not participate in the Japan selection trials for the 1984 World Judo Championships. Thus, they were effectively shut out from the championships. However, the Tokyo District Court accepted the judokas' damages claim against the federation for pain and suffering due to the imposition of the aforesaid qualification limits and ruled in their favour.[87]

81. *Court Act*, law no. 59 of 1947 and amendment law act no. 36 of 2006.
82. Supreme Court of Japan Judgment, 8 Sep. 1989 Civil Decisions Reporter (*Minshu*), vol. 43, no. 8, 889 (author's translation from Japanese).
83. Tokyo District Court Judgment, 25 Aug. 1994, Decision Times (*Hanrei Taimuzu*), vol. 885, 264.
84. Tokyo District Court Judgment, 4 Jun. 1993, Decision Reports (*Hanrei Jiho*), vol. 1436, 65.
85. Tokyo District Court Judgment, 6 Sep. 1988, Decision Reports (*Hanrei Jiho*), vol. 691, 236.
86. Tokyo District Court Judgment, 30 Jan. 2006; Decision Times (*Hanrei Taimuzu*), vol. 1239, 267.
87. Tokyo District Court Judgment, 25 Feb. 1988, Decision Times (*Hanrei Taimuzu*), vol. 663, 243.

172. Even if sports disputes are regarded as 'legal disputes', the settlement of sports grievances requires a high level of specialist knowledge that ordinary courts do not possess. Thus, there has been much judicial reticence in this field.

173. In Japan, all this led to the recognition of the need for a specialist Alternative Dispute Resolution (ADR) body to deal with sports disputes. Consequently, the first such body in Japan, the JSAA, was established in 2003. The JSAA was founded by the JOC, JSPO and JPSA.

A. Establishment of the JSAA

174. A major reason behind the establishment of the JSAA was a January 1998 report entitled 'The Anti-Doping System in Japan' by the 'Committee on the Anti-Doping System' which was jointly formed by the JOC and JSPO. The report identified that as swift judgments were demanded for doping issues, ordinary courts were not a suitable forum for resolving such issues. Rather, it stressed the need for sports-specific arbitration. This led to the JOC Sports Arbitration Research Group being set up in 1999.

175. It was during this process in the following year that the swimmer *Suzu Chiba* took the Japan Swimming Federation (JSF) to the Court of Arbitration for Sport (CAS) concerning her selection for the 2000 Sydney Olympics.[88] Despite this being a purely domestic dispute, the lack of a Japanese sports arbitration body forced *Chiba* to apply to the CAS in Switzerland. As a consequence, the athlete had to bear massive costs for the arbitration, including various translation expenses. This strengthened calls in Japan for the establishment of a speedy and efficient domestic sports arbitration body which in turn enhanced support for the JSAA.

176. In terms of *Suzu Chiba's* application to the CAS, JSF accepted the CAS as the forum to resolve the dispute, although, in the end, the athlete lost his case. However, in its judgment, the CAS identified certain obscurities in the JSF's basic Olympic selection criteria and ordered the federation to pay part of the arbitration costs accordingly.[89]

B. Arbitrations and Mediations Handled by the JSAA

177. There are five types of disputes handled by the JSAA.

---

88. The JSF website in Japanese is available at: http://www.swim.or.jp/.
89. CAS Judgment, 24 Oct. 2000, CAS 2000/A/278, available at: https://jurisprudence.tas-cas.org/Shared%20Documents/278.pdf.

1. Disputes Adjudicated by an Arbitration Panel Using Sports Arbitration Rules

178. These types of disputes involve the sports competitor filing his/her grievance against the relevant sports association to the JSAA in relation to a decision by the association (excluding decisions made by referees during competition/matches) concerning both parties (the competitor's application fee is JPY 55,000). Typical cases include disputes where athletes demand the revocation of unreasonable sanctions imposed by sports associations (including suspensions from competitions) and disputes relating to allegations of procedural impropriety in tournament selection decisions administered by sports associations.

179. As far as these types of disputes are concerned, the JSAA does not cover all sports associations. Article 3(1) of the JSAA Rules states the JSAA is restricted to only adjudicating on sports associations that fall under the auspices of the JOC, JSPO, JPSA, regional, prefectural and municipal athletic associations and organizations that are members, associate members or affiliates of such associations.

180. This particular type of arbitration process based on sports arbitration rules is central to the JSAA's role as the integral purveyor of ADR to the Japanese sports world. As this process concerns disputes over the decisions of sports associations, the issue arises in all cases as to whether these decisions should be revoked by the JSAA. This point was addressed in the JSAA's first arbitral award, the so-called *Weightlifting Incident*, where the panel stated:

> We recognize that the sports associations have a certain amount of autonomy. To that extent, the Japan Sports Arbitration Agency panel respects the decisions of domestic sports federations.[90]

181. The JSAA panel also stipulated the cases below in which it would revoke sports association decisions when the:

- rules themselves which the sports association's decision conforms to infringe the law or are highly unreasonable;
- sports association's decision infringes the rules of that association;
- sports association's decision is highly unreasonable even though it does not constitute an infringement of the association's own rules; and
- the process that leads to the decision is defective.

2. Arbitration under Sports Arbitration Rules Based on a Specific Arbitration Agreement

182. This arbitration process was introduced in 2004 for all sports disputes excluding those in section 3.I above. This arbitration is established based on the

90. JSAA arbitration Judgment, 4 Mar. 2003, case no. JSAA-AP-2003-001 (author's translation from Japanese).

Commercial Arbitration Rules of the Japan Commercial Arbitration Association. The kinds of disputes envisaged for this process include sports business disputes (covering conflicts between sports associations and sponsors and over tournament broadcasting rights) and disputes between famous athletes, sponsors and sports associations. In actuality, however, this arbitration process is used very little because in comparison with the type discussed in section 3.I, the costs are high and the recognition of this process itself is not so high.

3. Mediation under Sports Mediation Rules Based on a Specific Mediation Agreement

183. Mediation was introduced in 2006 following increased consultations in relation to disputes that were not suitable for the JSAA's arbitration processes. The principles and regulations utilized in this mediation process are not disclosed or publicized. Also, mediation is gradually being used to a greater extent as an alternative to the type of arbitration discussed in section 3.II above.

4. Arbitration under Sports Arbitration Rules for Doping Disputes

184. At the 33rd UNESCO General Conference meeting in Paris in October 2005, the 'International Convention against Doping in Sport' was adopted unanimously. Japan became a signatory to the convention on 27 December 2006 and implemented it on 2 February 2007.

185. The Japan Anti-Doping Agency (JADA),[91] a signatory to the UNESCO Convention, on 1 July 2007 implemented the 'Japan Anti-Doping Code (Version 1.0)', and on the same day, the JSAA 'Sports Arbitration Rules for Doping Disputes' came into force. The first arbitration case in 2008 concerned an administrative grievance against JADA which the plaintiff athlete lost.[92] Further, in response to the issuance of the Amended Japan Anti-Doping Regulations on 1 January 2015, JSAA also revised a portion of its Regulations on Arbitrations of Doping Disputes. These rules apply (Article 2) to appeals against decisions made by the following bodies under the Japan Anti-Doping Code:

(1) the JADA;
(2) the Japan Anti-Doping Disciplinary Panel;
(3) the JOC (a public interest foundation corporation);
(4) the JSPO (a public interest foundation corporation);
(5) the JSPO for the Disabled (a public interest foundation corporation);
(6) the Prefectural Amateur Sports Associations; and

91. The JADA website is available in Japanese at: http://www.playtruejapan.org/.
92. JADA arbitration Judgment, 10 Jun. 2009, case no. JSAA-DP-2008-001.

(7) the National Sports Federations.[93]

5. Arbitrations under Sports Arbitration Rules for Member Associations

186. This is a type of arbitration established in 2013 to enable JOC members to appeal a JOC decision (e.g., disciplinary decisions imposed on JOC members), against the backdrop of increased scandals of its member associations. Now, in addition to the JOC, the JSPO and the JPC have also implemented mechanisms to enable aggrieved members to file appeals against their organizations (i.e., JSPO or JPC). However, no one has taken advantage of such mechanisms to date.

Arbitrations under Sports Arbitration Rules for Governance Code for National Sport Federations Compliance Audits.

This is a type of arbitration established in 2021 to enable National Sport Federations to appeal a decision by a relevant governing body (i.e. JOC, JSPO, and JPSA) regarding their compliance audits based on the Governance Code for National Sport Federations (*see* paragraph 54).

187. Please note that in relation to the above ADR processes, emergency arbitration proceedings are provided in the cases of the types of arbitration in sections 3.I, 3.II, 3.IV, and 3.V. In principle, these proceedings are handled swiftly by a single arbitrator.[94]

C. Limits of the JSAA

188. Arbitration is an ADR process which requires all the connected parties to agree to use arbitration as the process to resolve disputes. It is also possible after a dispute arises for the athlete and sports association to agree to refer the case to the JSAA. There are examples of such cases but in practice securing such agreement is very difficult. Furthermore, it takes a lot of courage for athletes to bring dispute proceedings against sports association decisions. Often athletes can be reluctant to apply for arbitration itself due to the risk of it being rejected out of hand by the sports association.[95]

189. Therefore, in order to compel sports associations to become a party to JSAA proceedings when applied for by athletes, the JSAA has established an automatic arbitration acceptance provision in its 'Sports Arbitration Rules'.[96] The JSAA

93. JSAA, *Sports Arbitration Rules for Doping Disputes* (JSAA 2007), these rules are available in English at: http://www.jsaa.jp/sportsrule/index.html#02.
94. *Ibid., see* Art. 55(4).
95. Masato Dougauchi & Yoshihisa Hayakawa (eds), *An Introduction to Sports Law* 92 (Kyoto: Minerva Shobou Ltd., April 2011).
96. Masato Dougauchi, *A Consideration and Summary of the Main Points Concerning the First Three Years of the Japan Sports Arbitration Agency*, in *Towards Further Development in Sports Arbitration* 7 (Sophia Law School, March 2006).

has carried out activities to ask sports associations to publicize this provision to athletes, but these have not yielded desirable results. Owing to the steady educational efforts of the JSAA, there has been an increase in the use of automatic consent of arbitration clauses. However, there are still many sports associations that resist having their decisions reviewed by external dispute resolution bodies and which insist that disputes can only be handled through their internal grievance mechanisms.[97]

190. According to data collated by the JSAA as of 6 July 2021, out of the sixty-six sports associations and affiliated associations in the JOC, sixty, including JOC, have adopted the provision (91%). Also, out of the ten sports associations and affiliated associations in the JSPO, eight, including JSPO, have adopted the provision (80%). Regarding sports associations and affiliated associations within the JPSA, only twenty-six out of forty-six have adopted the provision (56%). Regarding sports associations and affiliated associations within the Prefectural Amateur Sports Associations, only thirty-four out of forty-seven have adopted the provision (72%).[98]

191. Even when an athlete has the courage to apply for arbitration, there is no end to the number of sports associations that will reject initiating such proceedings in the first place. In fact, there is an abundance of examples where sports associations have refused to accept arbitration. These include the 2003 *Boxing Incident* (where a boxer applied for the revocation of deregistration sanctions, including a one-year prohibition on re-registration, imposed by the Japan Amateur Boxing Federation)[99] and the 2008 *Athlete Registration Incident* (where athletes demanded registration from bodies such as the Japan Industrial Track and Field Association).[100]

192. Another controversial example of this that whipped up a storm in the mass media was the 2007 *Kazuki Ganaha Incident*, where the J-League rejected *Ganaha's* (a football player) application for JSAA arbitration. In this dispute, the J-League club *Kawasaki Frontale* player *Ganaha* demanded the revocation of a league-imposed six-match suspension for an alleged breach of doping rules. Initially, *Ganaha's* desire was to have the arbitration held at the JSAA, but the J-League rejected this and announced that the case must be heard at the CAS. Therefore, the player had no other option but to file for CAS arbitration. In the end, *Ganaha's* case was accepted by the CAS, which ruled that the suspension should be revoked.[101]

193. Nevertheless, for the CAS arbitration, Ganaha bore a total of JPY 34 million in costs, which included expenses for translation, interpretation and expert witness statements. Had the J-League accepted arbitration at the JSAA, such massive

97. *Ibid.*
98. These data are available on JSAA website: http://www.jsaa.jp/doc/arbitrationclause.html (visited on 14 November 2021).
99. Tokyo District Court Judgment, 30 Jan. 2006; Decision Times (*Hanrei Taimuzu*), vol. 1239, 267.
100. A report of this incident is available in Japanese at: http://home.m07.itscom.net/jita/topics/pdf/20080125_a.pdf.
101. CAS decision, 26 May 2008, CAS 2008/A/1452, available at: http://jurisprudence.tas-cas.org/Shared%20Documents/1452.pdf.

costs would not have arisen. Moreover, the J-League drew stinging criticism from the mass media for its stubborn insistence on the CAS being the forum for the arbitration. It can be said that following *Suzu Chiba's* CAS arbitration in 2000, the problem has surfaced that players have to bear massive costs for such proceedings.

194. Thus, as aforementioned, in Japan, there remain a high number of sports associations that lack awareness of the concept of *swift and appropriate* dispute resolution. It was against this background that MEXT released its report on the strategy for national sports in August 2010. Article 4 of this report stipulates:

> It is required of sports associations that they demand the swift and smooth resolution of sports disputes. In order to promote development in effective dispute resolution systems, it is necessary to enhance the understanding of associations and athletes in dispute resolution procedures and also to cultivate the skills of arbitrators and mediators. On top of this, we support a strengthening in the functions of the Japan Sports Arbitration Agency.

195. Furthermore, Article 5(3) of the BSA places a duty on sports associations to strive for swift and appropriate resolution of disputes involving sports, and Article 15 provides that the state has various obligations in relation to guaranteeing the impartiality of arbitrations and mediations for such disputes. Recently, the JOC has made it an obligation for member associations to respond to arbitrations filed in accordance with JSAA rules and to announce this decision (Article 9.8, JOC Member Regulations[102]). JSPO has also made it an evaluation criterion for a sport's qualification for the National Sports Festival whether a sports organization implements the JSAA automatic arbitration consent clause or not.[103] Even the JSAA itself mentioned the importance of the independence and impartiality of the dispute resolution chamber as well as the automatic arbitration consent clause in its publication 'Fair Play Guidelines for NF Organizational Operations' in 2014, in the chapter of 'the Construction of Penalty System and Dispute Resolution System'. Also, as mentioned above, the newly published 'Governance Code for National Sport Federation Members' (*see* paragraph 54) requires national sports federations to use JSAA as a dispute resolution body.

196. Thus, as a result of these provisions and efforts, it is widely expected that the sports associations will further develop their dispute resolution bodies, which will lead to swifter and more appropriate settlement of sports disputes.

102. At https://www.joc.or.jp/about/regulation/pdf/kameidantai.pdf.
103. At http://www.japan-sports.or.jp/Portals/0/data/kokutai/doc/kitei22.pdf (only available in Japanese).

Part II. Sport and Employment

Chapter 1. General Issues

§1. Amateurism and Eligibility Issues

197. As aforementioned, *amateurism*, which Japan has since old times embraced, is highly prevalent in the sports world, with there being a long-standing period of almost no interaction between professionals and amateurs.

198. This is particularly the case in baseball, which was for a long time Japan's only professional league. In 1961, the relationship between professional and amateur sports worsened, when a professional baseball team midway through the amateur season plucked an amateur player and made him professional (this was named the *Yanagawa Incident* after the player *Fukuzo Yanagawa* who was plucked by the professional team). In fact, this incident virtually severed relations between professional and amateur sports for a prolonged period.

199. To be more precise, not only did the regulations prevent professionals and amateurs from playing matches and training together but also there were severe restrictions imposed on players with professional experience in returning to the amateur game. As a matter of course, professional players were forbidden to make a comeback in amateur baseball. In fact, even to become a student baseball coach following retirement as a professional player, such players had to first be a school teacher for over ten years. Thus, due to the imposition of such harsh restrictions, it was virtually impossible to become a student coach. For instance, in order to become a school teacher, it was necessary to get a teaching certificate; so for players that turned professional following high school graduation, they had to begin studying for this certification from scratch after retiring. Therefore, it essentially required more than a decade, post-retirement, to become a student coach.

200. These harsh restrictions effectively closed the door to professional players post-retirement, who wanted a second career as either an amateur team or university or high school coach. On top of this, even university and high school baseball players lost out as it became apparent they could not receive lessons from these current or former professional players. This situation continued for over forty years following the *Yanagawa Incident*, at which point the regulations became gradually more relaxed.

201. In particular, from 1999, former professional players were permitted to enter amateur baseball teams belonging to the JABA,[104] at a rate of up to two such players per team per season (it has been increased to three players now). By the same token, reforms were enacted in 2002 which made it possible for former professionals that played with JABA amateur teams for more than two years to rejoin professional teams.[105]

202. In order for former professional players to become student baseball coaches, in 1997 the condition that the said player had to work 'post-retirement for over ten years as a school teacher' was relaxed to 'over two years'. However, due to the burden of having to acquire teaching certificates as discussed above, there have only been less than thirty former players who became student baseball coaches in the last thirty years. In this big environment, the JPBPA has organized exchange events for professional players and student players since 2000 to promote interactions and discussions. Since April 2010, the regulations that had in principle prohibited interaction between professionals and amateurs underwent a major revision in the form of the Japan Student Baseball Association's (the association for high school and university baseball) Japan Student Baseball Charter (JSBC), which generally made such interaction acceptable again.[106] Further, since the start of the Student Baseball Eligibility Resumption System in 2013, the returning to student baseball eligibility by professional players has become widely recognized.

203. In football, both the professional and amateur games are unified under the JFA,[107] with the net result being much successful interaction. Nevertheless, in other sports, there is often a separation between amateurism and professionalism based on strict amateur regulations.

204. Golf is an example of this type of model.

205. Amateur regulations even exist in boxing, where in the past, for example, an amateur boxer in his junior high school years had a one-year suspension imposed on the grounds of participating in a pro-exhibition bout. Consequently, in September 2003, as the boxer was unable to enter the All Japan Inter High School tournaments, he filed a case with the Tokyo District Court demanding the reversal of the suspension and JPY 500,000 in damages for pain and suffering. On 30 January 2006, the court dismissed the boxer's case;[108] however, the boxer appealed and the parties later reached a settlement.

---

104. The JABA website in Japanese is available at: http://www.jaba.or.jp/.
105. Please refer to the JABA rules, available in Japanese at: http://www.jaba.or.jp/gaiyou/kitei/touroku.pdf.
106. The Japan Student Baseball Association in Japanese is available at: http://www.student-baseball.or.jp/.
107. The JFA website in English is available at: http://www.jfa.or.jp/eng/index.html.
108. Tokyo District Court Judgment, 30 Jan. 2006; Decision Times (*Hanrei Taimuzu*), vol. 1239, 267.

206. In other sports, amateur regulations exist in sumo wrestling to prevent wrestlers who have achieved above a prescribed ranking from returning to amateurism. In Judo, there are regulations which stipulate that professional fighters from other combat sports cannot register as amateur judokas until three years after their retirement from the said sport (one year in the case of registering as an instructor).

§2. Student Athletes Issues

I. High School Baseball Scholarship Issue and the JSBC

207. As aforementioned, the student sports system has massively supported sports in Japan, including through *Koshien*, the national high school baseball tournament that grabs the attention of the whole country. Therefore, the student sports system still has significant meaning.

208. To illustrate this, there are some private schools within the high school system that establish strong baseball teams to actively participate in the *Koshien*. By doing this, the schools want to create a positive advertising effect, through which they can raise their profiles and therefore increase the number of applicants who want to enter. Furthermore, in order to attract excellent junior high school baseball players, such schools also provide economic privileges in the form of student scholarship packages that include exempted tuition and accommodation fees.

209. It was often suspected that students who received such economic privileges in the form of tuition, living expenses and other cash or gifts, did so on the grounds that they were players or team members, which was prohibited under Article 13 of the former JSBC. In reality, however, such support was tacitly provided for a long period.

210. In 2007, the *Seibu Lions*, a professional baseball team, was discovered to have handed over so-called *bribes* to parties such as university baseball players (it is prohibited under the JSBC for professional baseball teams to provide amateur students with such types of financial *bribes*). It became clear that when the student concerned had entered high school, he was a scholarship student, through which his tuition fees were exempted due to his sports performances in junior high school. This became a big issue as it was a violation of the JSBC. As a consequence of strict questioning from the Japan High School Baseball Federation (this is also known as the *Koyaren*), the high school in question took responsibility and dissolved its team.[109] A major social problem developed from the resulting fall-out.

211. The strict stance that the *Koyaren* took towards this type of student scholarship problem met with much criticism, as it was not prohibited in other sports,

109. The Japan High School Baseball Federation website in Japanese is available at: http://www.jhbf.or.jp/.

including football. The federation was further rebuked because its stance to suddenly discard the scholarship system ignored the situation that many scholarship students were actually entering famous baseball high schools. Criticism also mounted that discarding the scholarship system was unreasonable because it forced many students to quit their schools and move to new ones.

212. In the end, the High School Student Baseball Scholarship Problem Advisory Committee was formed in relation to this matter. Following its deliberations, the committee decided that scholarship students could be accepted provided certain conditions were applied. Basically, scholarship students were to be judged against the same academic standards as regular students in the same school year. On top of this, scholarship students had to become *model students* with regard to their attitudes and behaviour. Furthermore, it was recognized that students should not be accepted as scholarship students simply on their baseball ability alone.

II. Wide-Ranging Revisions to the JSBC and New Developments Concerning the School Sports System and Amateurism

213. Originally in the school sports system, what was the logical reasoning to establish a system based on amateur regulations?

214. In Japan, hardly any clear theoretical debate has been held regarding this point. Consequently, there has been a tendency on occasions in amateur sports, based on the imprecise regulations of *amateurism*, to go beyond a reasonable extent in carrying out regulations.

215. Following these traditional conventions for amateur athletes, a theoretical explanation for the content of amateur regulations was attempted since April 2010 when the new JSBC came into effect. The revision of the JSBC was instigated by the aforementioned scholarship problem, where the need for such scholarships was examined. This examination was conducted by influential figures on the aforesaid advisory committee and resulted in the first big revisions being carried out to the charter since 1946.

216. The new JSBC represents a full-fledged revision of the previous charter, where the purpose was to *control* student baseball through *top-down regulations*. The new JSBC drastically re-examined this thinking by changing the focus of the student baseball framework to *student rights* through implementing *bottom-up regulations*.[110]

217. The quality of such student rights is enshrined in Article 26 (the right to be educated) of the Constitution of Japan. The position in accordance with this article is that there must be a clear demarcation between *professionalism* and *amateurism*

110. Please refer to the charter available in Japanese at: http://www.student-baseball.or.jp/kenshou/kenshou.html.

because of the need for education. Therefore, as a consequence, a theoretical explanation is being provided regarding the need for amateur regulations.

218. In other words, to prevent the true meaning of *education* from being threatened, this must be done through uniform regulation. Therefore, *professionalism* and *amateurism* are separated through the need to guarantee the above *right to be educated*. Additionally, the new JSBC is centred on the basic philosophy of *student rights*. The charter, even in relation to adverse dispositions, such as disciplinary punishments, stipulates procedural and human rights guarantees, including the improvement of dispute resolution bodies and the impartiality of their procedures to provide due process.

219. In the advanced sports law countries of Europe and North America, it is common for the rights of athletes and due process to be guaranteed by impartial dispute resolution bodies. However, in Japan, where a hierarchical sports culture still remains, such guarantees have yet to be realized even in professional sports.

220. The new JSBC, as well as establishing an internal dispute resolution body for the student baseball associations, also provides recourse for appeals against this body to the JSAA. Thus, even within amateur sports, this emergence of the concept of athletes' and players' rights in regulatory form represents a major breakthrough.

III. Handling of Collective Responsibility

221. In Japan, particularly in the sports world, there are many disputes that are dealt with on the basis of *collective responsibility*. For instance, if one team member is disgraced, not only is that member disciplined (e.g., through suspension) but so are all the other team members who did not even participate in the misconduct. From the perspective of the rights of students to play sports, it is widely considered that the established practice of collective responsibility and sanctions, including imposing suspensions on full-teams, must be re-examined.

222. In amateur sports, assuming that innocent team members are suspended to take collective responsibility for the team, even if these members wanted to fight such punishments in many cases there are no means to facilitate this. Therefore, even at the amateur and school sports level, there is a need to establish and maintain impartial dispute resolution bodies, such as those stipulated in the new JSBC.

223. In Japan, the JSAA exists as the specialist arbitration body for sports. However, even if athletes apply to the JSAA to appeal sports association decisions, there are cases where these appeals procedures are halted due to the associations not providing their approval for these disputes to be resolved through this arbitration forum. This, therefore, highlights the need to establish an impartial third-party body, as stated in the new JSBC, to which aggrieved athletes can appeal against such internal sports association decisions.

IV. Legal Position of Student Athletes

224. In Japan, there is also debate regarding the legal nature of the contract (including scholarships) between educational institutions and students, when the latter enter high schools or universities. In particular, when student athletes that enter universities or high schools, including on scholarships, cannot continue to compete in sports due to injuries, can educational institutions force these athletes to quit by cancelling their *student-school contracts*?

225. Another controversial matter is whether, even if student athletes are not forced to quit school, institutions can withdraw those athletes' benefits (including exempt tuition fees) so they are treated the same as regular students.[111]

226. On this point, concerning what kind of legal relationship develops in such situations, it is commonplace that no written contracts are exchanged between educational institutions and students. In these types of *student-school contracts*, the legal relationship is often imprecise. However, in practice, even if an athlete's sporting career is finished, this is rarely viewed by an educational institution as a case in which to force the athlete to quit.

227. It could occur that an educational institution forces an athlete to quit, by terminating their *student-school contract* on the grounds that the athlete's sporting career has finished. However, even in such cases, legally it is considered that pursuant to Article 1(3) of the Civil Code, there is a high possibility that the termination itself could be interpreted as 'void' due to an abuse of the right to terminate.

228. On most occasions when an athlete's sporting career comes to an end, it is not rare to find cases where the privileges the athlete has received up until that point, including tuition fees, are re-assessed by the institution. Furthermore, legally speaking, if the detriment to the athlete is only to that extent, it is considered reasonable.[112]

§3. Issues Concerning Semi-professional Athletes

I. Issues Concerning the Position of Athletes in the Corporate Sports System

229. As aforementioned, the *corporate sports system* in Japan strongly embraced amateurism up until the end of the 1980s. Here, the underlying public perception was that, as dictated by amateur regulations, it was necessary for employees to use their leisure time to play sports. Accordingly, the legal position of the players

111. Shu Suzuki, *Student Athletes: Special Admission on the Sport Quota and Duties under the Educational Agreement* 79 (Annual Review no. 9) *The Legal Problems Facing Amateur Sports* (Japan Sports Law Association, 2002).

112. *Ibid.*

and athletes was the same as that for other regular company employees. In other words, the athletes' sporting activities did not provide 'labour' and they were actually employed by the company under the same employment contracts (labour contracts) as regular employees.

230. However, as the concept of amateurism disintegrated and sports associations began to accept professionalism, the number of temporary employment contracts, which recognized sporting activities as the main provision of labour, increased dramatically.[113] Basically, it is not in doubt that athletes who provide labour like regular employees and who compete in sport merely when required are 'workers'. Nevertheless, when the contract for providing labour is mainly in the form of providing activities as an athlete, can this be called an 'employment contract?' This is because problems arise in the consideration of whether such athletes are 'workers' or not, as this will determine if they are protected under Japan's labour laws. As is addressed below regarding the long-standing debate in Japan on professional athletes as 'workers', in general, these parties are not covered by labour laws, which create big problems.

231. A 'worker' under Article 9 of the Labour Standards Act (LSA) is defined as, 'a person who is employed at an enterprise or place of business and receives wages, regardless of the kind of occupation'.[114] This definition of 'worker' is also the same in the Industrial Accident Compensation Insurance Act (IACIA) and the Minimum Wages Act (MWA).[115,116] Correspondingly, in determining whether or not the term 'worker' applies in these cases, in general, an assessment of various factors needs to be made (including, if there is the freedom to accept or decline the work, and also if commands are given in relation to the work).

232. Bearing this in mind, it is not only those athletes who provide regular labour that should be construed as 'workers' but also those whose main work involves sporting activities. Therefore, if corporate sports athletes are to be considered as 'workers', they will be subject to Japan's labour relations laws. From the perspective of the LSA, there are restrictions on the length of labour contracts, with Article 14 stipulating, 'No labour contracts … shall have a term of over three years.'

233. In relation to dismissal of employment, Article 16 of the Labour Contracts Act (LCA) stipulates that 'dismissal shall, where the dismissal lacks objectively reasonable grounds and is not considered to be appropriate in general societal terms, be treated as a misuse of that right and invalid'.[117] Thus, for instance, according to

---

113. Sasakawa Sports Foundation, *Sports Paper: The Future Direction for Sports* 129 (2011).
114. *Labour Standards Act,* law no. 49 of 1947 and amendment law no. 147 of 2004.
115. *Industrial Accident Compensation Insurance Act,* law no. 50 of 1947 and amendment law no. 111 of 2007.
116. *Minimum Wages Act,* law no. 137 of 1959.
117. *Labour Contracts Act,* law no. 128 of 2007.

this, it is difficult for a business executive who cuts a corporate sports team due to the poor performance of the corporation to use that as grounds for wanting to sack the players in the team.

234. There are also further issues in relation to the working-hour regulations. Article 32 of the LSA stipulates that in principle the working week should be 'forty hours' with not more than 'eight working hours per day'. Therefore, if sporting activities are considered labour (including matches and practice/training), then it is necessary that an athlete's working hours shall be within the aforesaid time range.

235. In applying the IACIA, particularly for athletes on regular labour contracts (contracts where provision of labour is the same as that for regular employees, and which the athlete uses the accompanying 'leisure' and 'welfare benefits' for their sporting activities) who get injured during the course of sporting activities, the problem arises as to whether such athletes are eligible for accident compensation insurance.

236. Namely, to receive such insurance, it is necessary for the injury or sickness to have been caused by a 'work' accident. The issue then becomes whether the sporting activities as 'leisure' and 'welfare benefits' can qualify as 'work'.

237. In May 2000, the MHLW (now called the Department of Labour) released its report entitled 'Recognition of Accidents that are Associated with Sports outside the Workplace'.[118] The report stipulated the following standards.

238. First, it distinguishes between external sports competitions and those held within work. In relation to the former, the prerequisites for an external competition to be considered as 'work' are that: (1) entry to the competition is treated as a business trip or attendance at work; and (2) the costs (including travel expenses) to enter are not borne by the worker. In relation to the latter, the prerequisite conditions that competitions held within work are to be considered as 'work' are that: (1) the objective of the competition is to have all workers from the same workplace or company participate; and (2) absence from the competition is treated as an absence from work.

239. Second, with regards to training to be considered as 'work', this shall be done according to the 'training plan' pre-determined by the employer. It is also necessary that the practice times, venue and content of the training are defined in the 'training plan' (however, the workers can be given the discretion by the employer, within a pre-determined limit, to amend the 'training plan').

240. If the above standards are fulfilled, athletes who have suffered an injury, sickness or accident in a corresponding match/competition and/or training, shall be eligible to receive accident insurance benefits.

118. MHLW, *Recognition of Accidents That Are Associated with Sport Outside the Workplace* (MHLW 17 May 2000, Report no. 366).

241. As an example concerning external sports competitions, in August 1990, there was a case where three athletes belonging to a food manufacturing company team were selected to represent Japan. These athletes died in a traffic accident while on the way to a Japan team training camp which led to the issue as to whether this qualified as a 'work accident' in terms of accident insurance benefits.

242. The Central Labour Standards Council denied claims from the bereaved athletes' families for these insurance benefits.[119] However, these decisions were overturned following an appeal by the families to the Labour Insurance Appeals Committee, which recognized that the traffic accident was a 'work accident'.[120]

243. Therefore, under the above MHLW standards which were announced following the Labour Insurance Appeals Committee judgment, it is considered at present that factually similar cases would probably qualify for accident insurance benefits. However, when assessing these MHLW standards, given the number of athletes who have executed professional contracts within the corporate sports system, caution should be applied in classifying such parties as 'workers' in the sense originally envisaged by the IACIA. This is because as previously mentioned concerning the debate in Japan on professional athletes as 'workers', in practice, under the IACIA, these parties are not treated as 'workers'.

II. Issues Concerning Restrictions on Player Transfers

244. When players in the corporate sports system wanted to transfer to another team, they were faced with restrictions from each relevant sports association. Some of these associations used to make it a requirement that a player's previous club's written approval has to be acquired for the player to transfer and that if the previous club's approval is not acquired, the player in question cannot compete for his new club for a set period (e.g., one year).

245. For instance, in corporate amateur athletics, an athlete could not transfer to a new team unless he/she has a release certificate approved by the old company team's division head and coach. However, even when the athlete has this certificate, he/she could not compete for his/her new team for six months from the date of that team's registration application.

246. These types of regulations were intended to prevent players from being poached. However, from the perspective of a player's freedom to choose his/her employment, the issue arises as to whether this can be considered a reasonable restriction. That is why JFTC has launched an investigation into the regulations above in terms of possible violation of antitrust laws and many of such regulations have been abolished after that.[121]

---

119. Central Labour Standards Council Judgment nos 221, 223, and 225 of 1993.
120. Labour Insurance Appeal Committee Judgment, 1996.
121. https://www.jiji.com/jc/article?k=2018122106518&g=eco.

III. Issues Concerning the Contracts of Coaches and Managers

247. There are often issues regarding the legal position of managers and coaches in the corporate sports system. For instance, there are cases when corporate team coaches who have employment contracts with the corporation can be removed from the role of coach and placed in another post by the employer.

248. There is a judicial precedent in Japan which stipulates that, in general, to change the role of a worker whose job requires a high level of specialist expertise; it is necessary to get that worker's approval.[122] Therefore, if a coach or manager is made to quit their role for another work post unless it is separately stated in the employment contract, this change cannot be facilitated without the individual's approval.

249. In October 2009, the coach of the Nagoya Sangyo University baseball team received a notice from the university that he was being transferred from the role of a coach to the employment bureau. The coach, alleging that the notice violated his employment contract, subsequently applied to have his case heard at the Nagoya District Court Labour Tribunal (please note that the parties later reached a settlement).

122. Fukui District Court Judgment, 27 Mar. 1987, Decision Times (*Hanrei Taimuzu*) vol. 641, 115.

Chapter 2. Sources of Employment Law

§1. Legal Status of Players

I. Professional Sports Players and Athletes as Workers

250. One thing that has long been debated in Japanese professional sport is whether it can be said that professional sports players are 'workers' under the related Japanese labour law and legislation.

251. For instance, it is not doubted that parties such as professional golfers and athletes, who are independent and lead professional lives based on revenue from prize money and sponsorship, are 'sole-proprietors'. However, what is the situation when professional athletes, such as baseball and football players, belong to professional clubs and provide services under the orders of these clubs (including for training and match participation)?

252. Are the contracts between these players and clubs not considered 'employment contracts' under the Civil Code (Articles 623–631) or 'labour contracts' under the LCA? In other words, the issue is whether the legal status of these professional athletes is that of 'workers'.

253. The merit of debating this issue is the following point: Does labour law in Japan (including, the LSA, Labour Union Act (LUA), and IACIA)) apply to professional baseball and football players?[123]

254. In relation to this point, there seems to be a conflict between the *employment contract theory* for 'workers' and the *service contract theory* for 'sole proprietors'. It has to be noted that there is a difference between the definition of the term 'worker' in the LUA and 'worker' in the LSA and the IACIA. Due to the more extensive interpretation afforded to 'worker' in the former case, it becomes necessary to reconsider the application of the term for each piece of legislation, respectively.

II. 'Workers' under the LUA and Professional Sports Players and Athletes

255. First, 'workers' under Article 3 of the LUA are defined as 'those persons who live on their wages, salaries, or other equivalent income, regardless of the kind of occupation'.

123. *Labour Union Act,* law no. 174 of 1949 and amendment law no. 87 of 2005.

256. Professional baseball players formed the JPBPA, which acquired certification as a labour union from the Tokyo Labour Relations Commission (TLRC) in 1985. Therefore, at the very least, there is no doubt that these players will be regarded as 'workers' under the LUA.

257. In fact, when the JPBPA held its strike in 2004, the NPB clubs asserted that the players were not classified as 'workers' under the LUA. However, this assertion was rejected when the Tokyo District Court confirmed that professional baseball players under the Act were 'workers'.[124] Furthermore, when the NPB did not hold negotiations in good faith with the JPBPA in March 2002, the association claimed legal redress against unfair labour practices based on the LUA to the TLRC. In the proceedings, the commission went through the procedure on the basis that the players were 'workers' (a settlement was reached between the parties in March 2004).[125]

258. Furthermore, the JPFA received union certification from the Tokyo Metropolitan Government Labour Relations Commission in September 2011.[126] Although there are certain differences in the working environments between professional football players and professional baseball players, the fact that the JPFA gained union certification means that professional football players are recognized as 'employees', at least from the labour union law perspective.

III. 'Workers' under the LSA and the IACIA and Professional Sports Players and Athletes

259. A 'worker' under Article 9 of the LSA is defined as 'a person who is employed at an enterprise or place of business and receives wages, regardless of the kind of occupation'. This definition of 'worker' is also the same in the IACIA and the MWA. Correspondingly, in determining whether or not the term 'worker' applies in these cases, in general, an assessment of various factors needs to be made (including, if there is freedom to accept or decline the work, and also if commands are given in relation to the work).

260. From this perspective, it seems that there is no reason for professional baseball and football players to be excluded from the term 'worker' under the LSA. However, those players have not been treated as 'workers' in the sense that it is defined under the LSA. Please note that to date, there has been no specific court judgment on this point. It is possible that in the future a court may judge professional baseball players or footballers to be 'workers' under the Act.

124. Tokyo District Court Judgment for Preliminary Injunction, 3 Sep. 2004; Tokyo High Court Judgment for Preliminary Injunction, 8 Sep. 2004 (please *see* Keiji Kawai, *A Consideration of the Japan Professional Baseball Players Association's Strike – The Legal Rights of Professional Baseball Players*, *Legal Classroom* no. 291, 4 (Yuhikaku Publishing Co., Ltd., 2004).

125. *Ibid.*

126. The JPFA website in Japanese is available at: http://www.j-pfa.or.jp/.

261. Up until now, the main reason that those players are not treated as 'workers' as defined by the LSA is that the Act's chief purpose is to provide regulations for industrial workers (including for working hours) and not to control specialist professions such as baseball players. Therefore, it is widely believed that it is out of place to apply this Act to professional athletes as 'workers'.

262. However, at present, it has to be noted that as work arrangements diversify, the number of regulations for specialist professions is increasing, even within the LSA. Therefore, it is quite possible that these regulations and the Act will apply in some part to professional sports players.

§2. Employment Relationship

263. As a general rule, the contracts entered into between players and clubs in professional sports such as baseball and football, are uniform contracts formulated by the relevant leagues and sports associations (separate agreements are also made by the parties to cover individual circumstances). Accordingly, it is frequently the case that the scope of negotiation between the players and clubs is limited.

264. In such uniform contracts, it is often determined that the regulations of the sports associations to which the clubs belong must be strictly complied with. It is almost always the case that such regulations are structured not to allow any direct engagement with the players. This is in pure contrast to the situation in America, where the labour agreement process is more disciplined because the players' associations possess exclusive bargaining power in connection to players' working conditions. Therefore, many parts of the players' contracts are determined through mutual negotiation between the clubs and players' associations.

265. In Japan, because the form and content of these player contracts are so unbalanced, it is often asserted that these so-called uniform contracts (or contracts of adhesion) can be invalid for abuse of a dominant position under antitrust law (Article 90 of the Civil Code).[127] In particular, the bargaining power of players in professional baseball is greatly restricted by both the amateur draft system and the reserve system. There is much vigorous debate in connection with the legal validity of such restrictive trade practices.

266. In football, there is an active movement towards establishing a minimum level of players' rights at the world level. This is illustrated through FIFA in its Circular no. 1171 of 24 November 2008 concerning uniform player contracts.[128] These minimum requirements include guaranteeing players' image rights, paid holidays and players' right to seek second or third opinions from specialist medical practitioners in case there are differing opinions between the club and the player.

127. Masaji Chiba & Yoshio Hamano (eds), *An Introduction to Sports Law* 11 (Taiiku Shisetsu Shuppan Ltd., December 1995).
128. *See* FIFA Circular no. 1171.

267. In comparison to the situation in baseball and football, in the world of martial arts and combat sports, there are many associations not belonging to other confederations and leagues. For this reason, within such associations, there is often a wider scope for individual bargaining between the parties to incorporate essential provisions into athletes' contracts.

§3. Fundamental Rights and Obligations for Clubs and Players

I. Baseball

A. System Based on the American Model of Baseball

268. The NPB, Japan's representative professional baseball league, is established based on the *American model of baseball.* Correspondingly, the NPB is operated on a *tightly controlled socialist economic* model. This model is epitomized by the *reserve system* (under the reserve system, clubs can unilaterally renew the players' contracts, and players cannot transfer to new clubs without the approval of their current club) and the *amateur draft* (under the draft, rookies only have the right to bargain with one club and cannot engage in negotiations with other clubs), where the players' freedom to select clubs is restricted, the entry of new teams is limited and the clubs have regional monopolies. The intention of these systems is to ensure a balance of strength and revenues among the teams.

269. This shall be contrasted below to Japan's other main professional sports league, the J-League, which is based on the *European model of football* and operated on a *capitalist/free market economic* model.

270. Currently, there is much debate in Japan on the various legal issues related to professional baseball, similar to those in America's Major League Baseball (MLB),[129] where the players have fought against the reserve system through labour disputes and litigation. These issues are examined below.

B. Restrictions on Rookies Entering Clubs: The Amateur Draft and Related Matters

271. It has been an established principle in the NPB since 1965 that clubs would sign amateurs and rookies who came through the draft. In relation to the bargaining rights of rookies intending to enter the NPB, the draft imposes various restrictions, including that players can only negotiate with one of the twelve NPB clubs.

272. Throughout the years, the draft has been through a number of changes. At the time of writing – April 2019 – the amateur draft is based on the system (the

129. The MLB website is available at: http://mlb.mlb.com/index.jsp.

so-called *Waiver Draft*) whereby the lowest-ranked teams from the previous season get the best pick of the top-rated new rookies' pool. However, in the first pick, each team is allowed to pick its desired player. Once all twelve teams have made their desired picks (please note, some of the picks are in conflict), the players are then allocated by lot.

273. The so-called *alternating format* is then employed from the second pick which operates so that the lowest-ranked teams from the previous season get priority in the pick. The third pick then alternates so that the previous season's highest-ranked teams get priority. Similarly, the lowest-ranked teams get priority in the fourth pick and this *alternating format* continues until the conclusion of the draft.

274. This type of amateur draft was adopted based on the *rookie pool* system operated in America's National Football League (NFL). The purpose of this system is to guarantee equilibrium of power among the clubs and to prevent the runaway transfer fees that arise through teams fiercely competing to sign the best players. In connection with this, the compensation for rookies is capped at JPY 100 million for signing fees and at JPY 50 million for bonuses that are contingent on players' performances.

275. However, it has long been the case that violations of the maximum compensation caps are rife, in particular, there have been many instances of bribery. Bribes are paid in two different ways. The first way is for players to be paid more than the maximum signing fee when entering the team. The second way is for players at the rookie stage, prior to entering the team, to be paid set sums such as *training expenses*, which are in contravention of amateur association regulations, including the JSBC.

276. Fundamentally, under the amateur draft, teams that have the first picks do not need to compete with other teams to sign players; so it is unlikely that bribes have to be paid. However, even if a player is picked by a club in the draft, in the case he does not want to join that club, he can choose to reject it and continue his amateur career. For instance, the player may reject the club because he wants to put himself in a future draft to get a chance to be picked by his favoured team. If the player is still a high school student, he can do this by going to university or a corporate team. If he is already a semi-professional player, he can continue to play for a corporate team.

277. Correspondingly, in order to avoid being rejected in the draft, prior to making their picks, it is said that in practice the teams fight frantically to sign the most promising players, including by paying bribes. The draft is held every year from 30 October until 22 November (Article 4 of the NPB Amateur Draft Regulations). In the draft, if a team that acquires negotiating rights with a rookie does not sign that player before the end of March in the following year, that team shall lose its negotiating rights (Article 11 of the NPB Amateur Draft Regulations). Please note, the equivalent rule for amateur players that belong to the JABA stipulates that the relevant club will lose its negotiating rights if the player does not sign before the end of January in the year following the draft.

278. Consequently, should a player reject a team, he can then be picked by a different team in the draft. However, according to Article 3 of the NPB Amateur Draft Regulations, certain restrictions apply in the event a player rejects a team and then enters a corporate baseball team. If that player is a junior high school/high school graduate or a university graduate, he is restricted from entering an NPB team for either three or two years, respectively.

279. Due to the proliferation of such bribery in Japanese baseball, the NPB has made clear its intention to stamp this problem out. It has facilitated this through establishing rules entitled the 'Rules on Signing Rookie Players: Infringements of the Rules and Related Sanctions'.[130] Nevertheless, with bribery being a long-standing custom in Japanese baseball, it is said that this proliferation will still continue because bribes are even being obtained by parties in amateur baseball, including coaches.

280. It has frequently become a subject of discussion that the amateur draft is unreasonable as it contravenes a player's constitutional right to freely choose his occupation (Article 22 of the Constitution of Japan). In particular, the *Egawa Incident* (as outlined in the 'The History of the Study of Sports Law in Japan' section above) prompted a wealth of debate even in the Japanese parliament about related legal issues. Embedded in that legal debate was the issue that an unreasonable contract, which contravenes a player's freedom to choose his occupation, is void as an act against public policy (Article 90 of the Civil Code). Another issue was that the NPB, as a trade organization, carried out unreasonable trade restrictions that contravened competition law (Articles 8(1) and 3 of the 'Act on Prohibition of Private Monopolization and Maintenance of Fair Trade', hereinafter the 'Anti-Monopoly Act').[131]

281. Nevertheless, the amateur draft is still in existence and there have been no challenges in the courts to the aforesaid legal issues (The issue of the amateur draft in relation to the application of the Anti-Monopoly Act will be examined below.).

282. In recent years, there have been cases where amateur players have skipped the NPB and signed contracts directly with American professional baseball clubs. Even in the MLB, the same draft system as in Japan has been introduced. However, the American draft does not prohibit MLB teams from freely signing Japanese players from outside the NPB draft system. This has created a source of tension for NPB clubs that have to compete vociferously to sign promising Japanese amateur players as they find it is massively difficult to overcome competition from the MLB clubs.

---

130. The rules are available in Japanese at: http://jpbpa.net/up_pdf/1284364723-534164.pdf.

131. *Act on Prohibition of Private Monopolization and Maintenance of Fair Trade*, law no. 54 of 1947 and amendment law no. 35 of 2005.

283. In autumn 2008, *Junichi Tazawa,* at the time with the Nippon Oil Corporation amateur team, wanted to challenge himself in the MLB, so he announced his intention to go to the MLB and asked all the NPB teams not to pick him in the upcoming NPB draft. This inevitably caused a great outcry in Japan at the time (please note that soon after this, *Tazawa* signed with the Boston Red Sox in December 2008).

284. In reaction to this so-called *Tazawa Incident,* the NPB acted to prevent promising Japanese amateur players from directly joining MLB teams without first going through the NPB by creating a new system. This system stipulated that Japanese amateur players who moved directly to foreign clubs were restricted for a certain period from signing contracts with NPB clubs after they left those foreign clubs (high school graduates for three years and university graduates/corporate amateurs for two years).

285. Parties such as the JPBPA heavily criticized these restrictions (so-called *Tazawa Rule*) as being a threat to and highly unreasonable for players who try to join MLB teams without first playing for their NPB counterparts. In 2020, JFTC launched an investigation into the system above in terms of possible violation of antitrust laws, and consequently, it has been abolished by NPB in September 2020.

C. Transfer Restrictions

1. Reserve System

286. As aforementioned, professional baseball in Japan was established based on the model adopted from America. Due to this, the reserve system as in the MLB has long been in effect to restrict the transfer of the top players. The reserve system is a system whereby NPB clubs can register certain players on a reserve list, and for as long as they remain on it these players cannot transfer to other clubs. Put another way, this is a system where the clubs can unilaterally renew a player's contract without even taking into account his intention or opinion to the contrary. In fundamental terms, once a player's contractual term (typically this is for ten months from February until November) with his club ends, he should be free to transfer to other clubs. However, as a result of the reserve system, this freedom is massively restricted.

287. In the MLB, to break down the reserve system, the players utilized various legal means such as litigation and arbitration. This led to the situation in 1976 where the players successfully gained the freedom to transfer (free agents) and thereby circumvented the reserve system.

288. Even in Japan where the reserve system has long been established, in 1993, free agency was introduced and a partial freedom to transfer became recognized. However, in truth, free agency became hampered by the two major points set out below:

(1) In order to be eligible for free agency, it is necessary for a player to be registered in the starting roster for a long period.
(2) The signing club must pay a huge compensation fee (the compensation fee can be wholly in money or money plus a trade of one of the players who is not listed on the twenty-eight man protected list of the transferee club).

Therefore, in practice, the freedom to transfer through the free agency system is significantly restricted.

289. As a consequence of this, the JPBPA announced that it would bring legal proceedings to fight this system in 2007. As a result of the negotiations between the NPB and JPBPA, partial reforms were carried out in favour of the players. The main points concerning the free agency system are set out below:

(1) To become eligible for free agency, a player must have been registered in the top team roster for nine seasons ('one season' is calculated as the player being registered for 145 days or more in the top team roster). Please note, the 2008 reforms mean that: (i) for domestic transfers between NPB clubs, the eligibility period was reduced to eight seasons; and (ii) when new players who joined NPB teams after the 2008 season were university graduates or corporate team players, the period for free agency eligibility was reduced to seven years for domestic transfers.
(2) When a player exercises his free agency right to transfer to a domestic NPB team, the signing club must pay the player's former club compensation. This amount of compensation was the equivalent of 120% of that player's previous year's annual salary from his previous club (in the case the transfer is in conjunction with a trade, then 80% of the player's annual salary was payable). However, this changed with the 2008 reforms, which are outlined below:
    (a) The amount of compensation is determined through a salary rank (excluding foreign players) at every club. Rank 'A' players are those ranked between 1 and 3 inclusive. Rank 'B' players are those ranked between 4 and 10 inclusive. Rank 'C' players are those ranked 11 and below.
    (b) Compensation payable for rank 'A' players is 80% of the player's previous year's annual salary, with the figure being 60% for rank 'B' players. For rank 'C' players, the compensation has been abolished (in the case a free agent transfers in conjunction with a trade, the amount of compensation payable is reduced for rank 'A' players from 80% to 50% of their previous annual salary, with the reduction for rank 'B' players being from 60% to 40%, accordingly).

290. By way of comparison, for players in the MLB to become eligible for free agency, they need to have been registered in the major team roster for just six seasons. Moreover, there are no compensation fees required (compensation is required in certain cases but the method of compensation is facilitated through the teams assigning their draft picks, which all teams receive regardless of their financial standing).

291. In Japan, there are various legal views espoused in relation to both the reserve and amateur draft systems.[132] First, it is often said that these systems along with the unreasonable players' contracts are void as acts against public policy because they contravene a player's freedom to choose his/her occupation.

292. Second, it is said that these systems act as unreasonable restraints on trade and thereby violate the Anti-Monopoly Act.

293. Third, it is asserted that these systems are void as they violate the regulations on the maximum duration for fixed-term employment contracts (according to Article 14 of the LSA, generally employment contracts shall not be concluded for a period exceeding three years or five years for certain professions) and also because they go beyond the reasonably accepted period in imposing a 'duty not to compete'.

2. Issues Concerning Foreign Transfers: The Posting System and Related Matters

294. As the NPB operates highly restrictive transfer and reserve systems, for players who have already joined NPB teams, no matter how they perform or even if they win the attention of MLB clubs, these players cannot transfer to foreign clubs.

295. Essentially, the reserve system is recognized based on an internal partnership agreement between the twelve NPB clubs, with the agreement only being valid in Japan. In the NPB, it is commonplace for clubs to conclude single-year contracts with players. However, these clubs, with only the protection of the said partnership agreement, take the risk that the players will be lured away by foreign clubs once their single-year contracts expire.

296. Therefore, in order to prevent individual players from transferring to the MLB and other foreign professional leagues in Korea, Taiwan and China, the NPB signed player contract agreements with each of these leagues (for instance, the NPB agreement with the MLB is entitled the 'United States – Japanese Player Contract Agreement' (US-JPCA)).[133] In accordance with these agreements, a player who is put on his club's reserve list cannot be signed by foreign clubs without the approval of the club.

297. Hence, if a Japanese player wants to transfer to an MLB club, as aforementioned he must first become eligible for free agency by spending nine seasons in the top team roster and then exercise his free agency rights abroad. The more highly skilled a player is, the greater the chances that the NPB clubs will do everything they can to keep the player. Thus, in practice, it is commonplace for the NPB clubs

132. Masaji Chiba & Yoshio Hamano (eds), *An Introduction to Sports Law* 11 (Taiiku Shisetsu Shuppan Ltd., December 1995).
133. The US-JPCA is available in English at: http://jpbpa.net/up_pdf/1284364663-401673.pdf.

not to grant a player permission to transfer to the MLB in the period prior to him becoming a free agent abroad, even if this is contrary to the player's wishes.

298. Please note that there are a few cases where NPB players have been able to negotiate free agent contracts with their clubs to transfer without cost to MLB clubs. Nevertheless, it has to be said that such cases are truly exceptional. On top of this, where free agents (e.g., players who have satisfied the nine-season top team roster requirement) have transferred to an MLB club, the transferor NPB club, unlike with domestic transfers, cannot demand a transfer fee from the MLB club. The reason for this is that in accordance with the agreement between NPB and MLB, MLB clubs are not obliged to pay transfer fees to NPB clubs. In other words, when free agent transfers occur, only the transferee NPB clubs are obliged to pay the transferor clubs.

299. Given the situation above, it goes without saying that NPB clubs want to 'sell' their players before they acquire free agent status, in order to get transfer compensation from MLB clubs. Basically, this entails selling the reserve rights of top players whom the MLB clubs may desire.

300. In fact, it occurs quite frequently that when an NPB club wants to sign a foreign player whose reserve rights are held by an MLB club, the NPB club pays the MLB club and in effect purchases the player's reserve rights (strictly speaking, the MLB club waives the player's reserve rights in return for payment from the NPB club). When considering this transaction in reverse, the NPB club could theoretically *sell* a player to an MLB club. However, in relation to the NPB clubs *selling* their top players to MLB clubs, there is a restrictive process called the *posting system,* which is stipulated in accordance with the agreement between NPB and MLB.

301. The posting system was first introduced in 1998. In the first era of this posting system (the 1998 Version of the posting system) from 1998 to 2013, the year in which the posting system was largely revamped, the process for auctioning players' reserve rights was similar to auctioning racehorses (blind bidding). Basically, it is a system that accepts the transfer process for players who want to transfer to MLB clubs and who still belong to NPB clubs. The system, however, did not allow the MLB clubs (thirty in total) to negotiate freely with such players, as it was in essence a bidding process held in relation to the posted player's reserve rights. The player and NPB club must then hold negotiations only with the MLB club who had made the highest corresponding bid.

302. Since the introduction of the posting system in 1998, the first Japanese player to transfer to an MLB club through this process was the famous Japanese player, *Ichiro Suzuki* (*Ichiro* transferred from the *Orix Blue Wave* to the Seattle Mariners in winter 2000).

303. The main reason for introducing the posting system was due to the troubled transfer of pitcher *Hideki Irabu* from the NPB *Chiba Lotte Marines* to the MLB in winter 1996. *Irabu* desired to move only to the New York Yankees; however, *Chiba* assigned the reserve rights of *Irabu* to San Diego Padres as they were in a business alliance, which gave the Padres exclusive signing rights to the player. *Irabu* strongly rejected signing for the Padres and in the end joined the Yankees following a trade between the teams. In response to this protracted transfer, various teams in the MLB vented their frustration at the lack of equal opportunities in such transfers.

304. In other words, many MLB teams decried the situation that only some of the thirty MLB teams could execute business alliance agreements with the twelve NPB teams for exclusive rights in signing Japanese players. This is because it was inevitable that a massive disparity would emerge between the teams that possessed such exclusive rights and those which did not. Therefore, the posting system was introduced in order to guarantee equal opportunities for MLB clubs in signing Japanese NPB players prior to them becoming free agents.

305. The various problems that have been identified with the 1998 version of the posting system are outlined below:

(a) It is a system that cannot be used unless the NPB club agrees to it in the first place, and no matter how much a player desires to transfer, he cannot unless the NPB club approves.
(b) NPB clubs have the power to reject the highest bid amount from the relevant MLB club. Also, no matter how much the player wants to move, the transfer can be rejected by the NPB club.
(c) Only the highest bidding club receives exclusive negotiating rights with the player, the player himself cannot freely choose the club he wants to transfer to.
(d) Only the highest bidding club receives exclusive negotiating rights with the player, so the player cannot negotiate with various clubs and about matters such as remuneration. It is, therefore, a completely detrimental system for the players.
(e) As the MLB team only needs to pay the amount of the accepted bid if they end up signing a contract with the player, it is possible for the MLB team to make a massive bid at the time of bidding. This can then have the effect of creating a bidding war and thus obstructing other MLB clubs in acquiring the player.

306. There were no negotiations at all with either the JPBPA or MLBPA in relation to establishing the 1998 version of the posting system as it was introduced unilaterally by the MLB and NPB.[134] In fact, the JPBPA in particular asserted that the system was illegal.

In this environment, MLB finally realized the problems of the 1998 posting system. In other words, a number of transfers highlighted the problem of skyrocketing bids by rich clubs which made it unfair for financially constrained clubs that could not compete with such bids. For instance, the bid price of the transfer of Daisuke Matsuzaka from Seibu Lions to Boston Red Sox was over USD 50 million; the bid price for the transfer of Yu Darvish from Nippon-Ham Fighters to Texas Rangers

134. The MLBPA website is available at: http://mlbplayers.mlb.com/pa/index.jsp.

also exceeded USD 50 million. Consequently, MLB and NPB started negotiations to reform this system. On the other hand, as a result of the joint effort to improve the situation between the JPBPA (who realized this problem from a long time ago) and the MLBPA, all MLB clubs that are willing to pay the amount designated by the NPB club, which cannot be more than USD 20 million, have gained the right to negotiate with the players since 2013:

(1) NPB teams must set their release fees (the fees that MLB clubs must pay NPB clubs for them to waive their reserve rights) at an amount less than USD 20 million and must notify the MLB of their release fees.
(2) The players may negotiate with any MLB clubs that are willing to pay the release fees. Once a player enters into a contract with an MLB club, the MLB club is required to pay the established release fee to the NPB club, and the NPB club is required to give up the reserve rights of the player.

Thanks to this new system, Issues C and D of the 1998 posting system as discussed above have been resolved. The new system is more advantageous to Japanese players.

The above system has been amended again in December 2017, where NPB teams can no longer set their release fees. Under the new system, the release fee is automatically determined based on the amount of the 'total guaranteed value' of the contract between the posted NPB player and the MLB club (15–20% of the 'total guaranteed value').

3. Trade System

307. As aforementioned, a trade system applies to the transfers of NPB baseball players. Basically, a trade is an act that transfers a player's reserve rights (also the player's contract based on his contractual status) from one club to another NPB club. Clubs can also make trades unilaterally without the player's agreement.

308. The trade system, when considering the players' contract from the perspective of employment contracts, is asserted as being void for contravening the provisions of Article 625(1) of the Civil Code, which states, 'An employer may not assign an employee's rights to third parties unless the employer obtains the employee's consent.'

309. Nevertheless, based on Article 21 of the NPB Uniform Player's Contract, the players comprehensively consent to their reserve rights being unilaterally transferred to the NPB clubs. Whether this type of *comprehensive agreement* is legally permissible has been the subject of much debate in light of the aforementioned Article 625(1) of the Civil Code.

II. Football

310. Along with baseball, Japan's other major professional sports league is the J-League. The J-League's structure follows the European football model (in particular Germany) which is operated on a *capitalist/free market economic* model. Therefore, unlike in baseball, the J-League has not established mechanisms such as the draft or reserve system to limit the freedom of players to select teams and also to restrict the entry of new clubs.

311. FIFA, football's global body, has implemented the FIFA rules for the governance of football worldwide. The rules established for governing football in Japan are fundamentally based on these FIFA rules. In 2001, FIFA reformed its rules and regulations to increase the freedom of players to transfer following the expiry of their contracts. Nevertheless, since this time, Japan has ignored the FIFA reforms, including formulating its own independent rules on domestic transfers. As a result, various legal issues have arisen which are addressed below.

A. *Transfer Restrictions*

312. In 1995, the European Court of Justice delivered the landmark *Bosman* ruling which literally shook the football world, especially in relation to the transfer of players.[135] In line with the *Bosman* ruling, FIFA reformed its rules and regulations in 2001, which provided the basis worldwide for the freedom of players to transfer.

313. Even in Japan, the rules were liberalized in line with the FIFA rules concerning international transfers. Therefore, players from Japanese clubs whose contracts had expired could transfer for free to clubs in foreign countries. However, in relation to Japanese players transferring abroad, this reform was a massive blow for the J-League clubs that had collected large transfer fees since Hidetoshi Nakata's 1998 transfer to *AC Perugia* in Italy's *Serie A*.

314. Even though the JFA liberalized matters concerning international transfers, it did not adopt the FIFA rules regarding domestic transfers until much later. Thus, even after a player's contract expired, domestic transfers for a long period still attracted fees based on a prescribed system of calculation, whereas there was no fee to sign for a foreign team.

315. In reaction to this, the JPFA sought FIFPro's support to remedy this inequitable domestic transfer situation. Consequently, JPFA's negotiations continued with the J-League, which led in 2009 to the long-overdue abolition of the domestic transfer fee system.[136]

135. ECJ, Judgment of 15 Dec. 1995, Case C-415/93, ECR 1995, I-4921.
136. Takuya Yamazaki. *Professional Baseball and Football Players' Rights and the Role of Lawyers in Japan. Liberty & Justice* 2009, August Issue (Tokyo: Japan Federation of Bar Associations, 2009).

316. Nevertheless, despite the JFA's abolition of this system, for domestic transfers, it now applies a training compensation fee which is more than twice that stipulated in the FIFA Circular no. 826 (31 October 2002).[137] This in turn has had the unfortunate consequence of creating a large obstacle to the domestic transfers of young players (under 23). The JPFA is currently demanding that this training compensation amount, which is in contravention of the FIFA rules, be remedied.

III. Basketball: B-League

317. In Japan, professional sports were centred on baseball and football for a long time. From 2005, however, the professional basketball league became independent of the Japan Basketball Association (JBA) and established the bj-league.

318. In opposition, the JBA continued to operate its own basketball league, which went through several name changes over the years, including the Japan Basketball League Organization (the former JBL), the Japan Basketball League (the new JBL since 2007), and the National Basketball League (NBL since 2013). As a result, Japan had two basketball leagues for ten years from 2005. The International Basketball Federation (FIBA) considered this situation problematic and thus banned the JBA from international games in November 2014. Therefore, the Japanese national basketball team was in peril of not being able to participate in the Rio de Janeiro Olympic Games Qualifiers that were going to be held in the second half of 2015. A discussion involving the MEXT came to the conclusion that the two leagues must be merged by the summer of 2015. In the fall of 2016, the Japan Professional Basketball League (B.League) was established as the new unified league under the auspices of the JBA. Based on the decision above, FIBA lifted the ban above, and therefore, the Japanese national basketball team has successfully participated in the Rio de Janeiro Olympic Games Qualifiers.

The main rules governing the contracts of B.League players are as follows.

Transfer Rules in B.League

(1) Once a player's contract ends, the current club will no longer have any reserve rights. The Player is free to transfer.
(2) The following transfer fees used to be applicable only to transfers from B2 (2nd division) to B1 (1st division), B3 (3rd division) to B1, and B3 to B2 until the end of the 2019–2020 season. The reasons for this rule were to prevent the drain of players to upper leagues, to maintain the strength of the teams and to mitigate the cost of new player acquisition to fill the gap left by the departing players.

137. FIFA Circular no. 826 on: 'Revised FIFA Regulations for the Status and Transfer of Players: Training Compensation' (Zurich: FIFA, 31 Oct. 2002), this is available at: http://www.fifa.com/mm/document/affederation/administration/ps_826_en_87.pdf.

a. Calculation of Transfer Fees

The base salary of the player in the previous season or the final amount offered for the next season by the former club during its negotiation with the player, whichever is lower.

b. Upper Limit of Transfer Fees

JPY 2.4 million.

Length of Contract

One- to three-year contracts.

Minimum and Maximum Salary

(1) The minimum salary of B1 clubs is JPY 3 million per annum (excluding consumption taxes); the minimum compensation of B2 clubs is JPY 2.4 million per annum (excluding consumption taxes).
(2) The maximum salary for rookies, in both B1 and B2 clubs, is JPY 4.6 million per annum (excluding consumption taxes).

IV. Boxing

319. In boxing, there were also restrictions on the freedom of boxers to transfer. Basically, in the event that the boxer wants to move from his/her current gym to another gym, he/she used to be obliged to submit a transfer request to the Japan Boxing Commission,[138] and it was necessary for that transfer request to be approved by the boxer's current gym. There were many cases where these gyms simply refused or demanded high fees for granting such approval. That is why JFTC launched an investigation into the restrictions above in terms of possible violation of antitrust laws. JBC decided to abolish it in 2019.

§4. Agents' Regulations

I. Situation Concerning the Player Agent and Management Business and Related Contracts

320. For many years in Japan, professional sports *agents* were alienated due to the assumption that they were the creators of distrust and miscommunication

138. The Japan Boxing Commission website in English is available at: http://www.jbc.or.jp/english/index.html.

between the clubs and players.[139] In fact, even in professional baseball, up until 2000, players had long been prohibited from requesting agents to negotiate contracts on their behalf with clubs (however, in that period, agents were permitted to conduct contract negotiations for foreign players).

321. From the J-League's inception in 1993, it was recognized that agents could conduct contract negotiations. In practice, however, due to some aforementioned Japan-specific conventions, for around ten years from 1993, there were very few players who utilized agents for negotiations. At the same time, today, the number of Japanese players transferring to foreign clubs is increasing and the sports business in Japan is modernizing, thus creating a greater awareness of players' rights. Consequently, as more players aspire to play abroad, there has been a gradual increase in the number of agents conducting negotiations for these players. Especially in football, transfers have become more active since the abolishment of transfer fees in 2009, and more players are using agents.

322. Moreover, there has been an increase in players' image rights management companies worldwide to cater for the media's demand for star players. In Japan too, this trend is apparent with the gradual growth of the agent and management business for Japanese players.

323. In Europe and America, it is common sense for players to outsource such agent and management issues to relevant service providers. By contrast, in Japan, in the sense that there are not so many players using agents, it can fairly be said that the agent and management business is still a work in progress. Although most J-League players use agents or intermediaries nowadays, the majority of professional baseball players still do not use agents.

324. Accordingly, as the professional sports industry for baseball and football in Japan matures, together with the expansion of a European-American style agent and management business, it is to be expected that trouble between such agents and players will increase (including matters involving exorbitant demands for commissions, fraud, embezzlement and neglect of accountability). From that standpoint, as with Europe and America which regulate such *agents* based on the law or internal sports association rules, Japan too is presently regulating agents on the basis of internal sports association rules.

139. Takuya Yamazaki & Shinsuke Ishiwatari, *The Process of Introducing the Professional Baseball Agent System: The Status of the Implementation and Future Players Expectations: And the Fight to Introduce the System and Future Issues. Liberty & Justice* 2001, September Issue (Tokyo: Japan Federation of Bar Associations, 2001).

II. Contents of the Agent and Management Service Business and the Agent System

325. The player *agent* business, namely the contents of the agent and management service business, is broadly categorized as below:

(1) Contract negotiations with clubs, transfer negotiations and negotiations in relation to the contents of player contracts.
(2) Management of players' image rights (media handling; public relations (including not only working to provide positive exposure in interviews and through establishing homepages but also providing risk/crisis management services like dealing with scandals); and negotiating advisory and related contracts with manufacturers for commercials, advertising, and various events).
(3) Management of players' financial matters, life-planning, and career support.
(4) Management in relation to miscellaneous player matters.

Although it is possible for one person or one company to handle such *agent* work, it is usually the case that many such parties cooperate on these matters.

326. Dependent on the nature and specialist field of the work in question, various agents, such as lawyers and management companies, can handle matters for players. In particular, management companies fulfil an important role for (2) and (4), and specialist tax advisers often deal with financial matters (3). Of these matters, the negotiation of player contracts (1) is at the core of services which *agents* provide to players. In Europe and America, this area of *agent* work is the main one which is subject to regulation.

327. In Japan, the JPBPA formulated Official Player Agent Regulations to govern agent activity in professional baseball. In professional football, agent activities were governed by the FIFA Regulations on Players' Agents (FIFA Agent Regulations) and the JFA Agent Regulations until March 2015. Since April 2015, the activities have been governed by the FIFA Regulations on Working with Intermediaries (FIFA Intermediary Regulations) and the JFA Intermediary Regulations. At present, there is still no such legislation at the national and regional levels. The specific content of these regulations mainly covers:

(1) restrictions of eligibility for agent certification;
(2) the legal obligations and prohibitions on agent activity; and
(3) disciplinary proceedings.

328. Regarding (1), in professional baseball, certified attorneys under the Japan Attorney Act are in practice the only parties who can conduct the work of players' agents. Although the JPBPA recognize not only such attorneys but also MLBPA certified agents as players' agents (Article 2 of the JPBPA Agent Regulations), the NPB clubs only recognize attorneys as agents on the grounds that Article 72 of the Japan Attorney Act prohibits non-attorneys from providing legal services. In professional football, anyone may work as an intermediary as long as he or she pre-registers to act as an intermediary and registers to provide representation in each individual transaction, provided that there are no special circumstances for the disqualification of such intermediary (Articles 3 and 4 of the JFA Intermediary Regulations, respectively).

329. Regarding (2), various regulations govern the obligations and prohibited activities of agents, such as the duty of confidentiality (Article 12 of the JPBPA Agent Regulations), reporting and written document submission obligations (Articles 17–24 of the JPBPA Agent Regulations). Also, the duty to submit agent contracts is covered by Article 14 of the JPBPA Agent Regulations, Article 6(1) of the FIFA Intermediary Regulations and Article 8(1) of the JFA Intermediary Regulations.

330. In relation to regulating the content of agent contracts, the length of these is restricted to a maximum of two years in professional football (Article 7(2) of the JFA Intermediary Regulations) and one year in professional baseball (Article 15 of the JPBPA Agent Regulations). There are no specific regulations concerning agent compensation; however, the JPBPA has issued agent compensation guidelines. In football, there are also benchmarks on monetary payments and limits on intermediaries' compensation (Articles 7(3) of the FIFA Intermediary Regulations and 9(3) of the JFA Intermediary Regulations). For example, an intermediary's compensation is recommended to be less than 3% of the player's compensation.

331. As noted above, in professional baseball, the NPB prohibits player agents from entering into contracts with multiple players. In actual fact, individual agents are limited to agreeing on an agent contract with only one player. Such agents are not restricted in representing both foreign and Japanese players together; however, they cannot represent multiple Japanese players at the same time. Therefore, in order for powerful agents to avoid such regulations, they introduce players to attorneys belonging to the same law office, who in turn represent those players.

332. The NPB has formulated these regulations as it is apprehensive towards powerful agents representing multiple players. However, there are no legal grounds to justify these unilaterally imposed regulations which are vehemently opposed by the JPBPA.

333. In fact, in 2001, the Japan Federation of Bar Associations wrote to the NPB about remedying these regulations. Even in professional football, there are no such regulations as individual player intermediaries can enter into intermediary contracts with multiple players.[140]

140. *Ibid.*

III. Actual Practice in Baseball

334. As a player cannot transfer under the reserve system until he acquires free agency rights, it is inevitable that agreements between the clubs and players are centred around single-year contracts (please note, however, there are cases where players who have either acquired or are acquiring free agency status agree to multiple-year contracts with their clubs). Accordingly, the players hold negotiations every year with the clubs to renew contracts. Two major issues exist in relation to renewing players' contracts.

335. First, most baseball players act by themselves and do not entrust agents to carry out contract renewal negotiations with the clubs. Moreover, until 1999, the NPB unilaterally prohibited players from using agents in such negotiations. For a very long period, the JPBPA called many times upon the NPB to lift these prohibitions on agents. However, no response whatsoever was forthcoming. This led to the JPBPA making the following assertion: 'Agent negotiations are not prohibited by law and it is not necessary to gain the club's approval in relation to these.'

336. Consequently, with the understanding that they did not require the approval of the clubs to legally introduce an agent system, the JPBPA from the 2000 offseason resolved to establish a system of registration, which they learned from the MLBPA. The NPB was subsequently notified of this. It was only with great reluctance that the NPB accepted the introduction of the agent system and subsequently dropped the restrictions on using agents from the 2000 offseason.[141]

337. Even following the lifting of agent restrictions, the NPB without the JPBPA's agreement unilaterally imposed further unreasonable restrictions, including: limiting each agent to representing only one Japanese player; and as a general rule, the player had to sit in with his agent for negotiations with the club. Due to these unreasonable restrictions which were agreed on and formulated by the NPB clubs, the present situation is that still very few players use agents for negotiations.[142]

338. Second, because the clubs were able to restrict the players' freedom through the reserve system, there was no concern about them transferring until these players became free agents. As a result, many players became highly frustrated at the paucity of their salaries in comparison to their market values. However, no matter how frustrated the players were with these salary offers, they had no choice but to accept these as they could not transfer to other clubs.

---

141. Takuya Yamazaki & Shinsuke Ishiwatari, *The Process of Introducing the Professional Baseball Agent System; the Status of the Implementation and Future Players Expectations*; *and the Fight to Introduce the System and Future Issues*, September Issue, Liberty & Justice 144 (Japan Federation of Bar Associations, 2001).

142. *Ibid.*

339. In relation to settling such salary disputes, a salary arbitration process has been made available. Nevertheless, the arbitrators for these salary arbitration hearings are selected by the commissioner, who is unilaterally selected by the clubs under the NPB's internal rules, which is highly inequitable. This point, therefore, illustrates the big problem concerning the impartiality of the dispute resolution body.

340. In practice, out of all the disputes that have been brought to the salary arbitration, there are no examples of such arbitrations which have fully accepted the claims of the players. Accordingly, for the players, this system is difficult to use.[143]

IV. Actual Practice in Football

341. The J-League was established in 1993 and from its inception was massively popular and seemed to be operating very smoothly. After this, however, problems began to emerge with match attendances falling, which led to the 1998 dissolution of the *Yokohama Flügels* and its merger with its cross-city rivals the *Yokohama Marinos* to form the *Yokohama F-Marinos*.

342. Following this incident, wide-ranging reforms were carried out to the system of J-League players' contracts. Basically, these reforms divided the players' contracts into three types: 'A' contracts, 'B' contracts and 'C' contracts. At the heart of these reforms were labour cost-cutting measures, which included limiting the number of 'A' contract players on annual salaries above JPY 4.6 million (excluding consumption taxes) to twenty-five players per team.

343. For new players, unless they had proven achievements such as being capped in a certain number of games by the Japan national team (including all national team levels, such as under-20s), they had to start from the 'C' contracts level (maximum annual salary of JPY 4.6 million). A rookie salary cap was also introduced, which meant that even players with proven achievements who joined J-League clubs on 'A' level contracts were subject to a maximum annual salary of JPY 6.7 million (excluding consumption taxes) in their first year.

344. By contrast, at around the same time, the first generation of agents based on the FIFA certified agents test began to emerge in Japan in 1998. Also during this period, *Hidetoshi Nakata* transferred to *AC Perugia* in Italy's *Serie A*, the league

143. Takuya Yamazaki, *Professional Baseball and Football Players' Rights and the Role of Lawyers in Japan*, August Issue, Liberty & Justice 63 (Japan Federation of Bar Associations, 2009).

where he was very successful. This signalled an increase in Japanese players transferring to foreign clubs, and at the same time attention began to focus on the activities of players' agents. Nowadays, almost all J-League players utilize the services of agents when negotiating with clubs.[144]

§5. Employment and Economic Dispute Settlement

I. Baseball

345. In the NPB, the arbitrators for salary arbitration hearings are selected by the commissioner, who is selected by the clubs, which is highly inequitable. This point, therefore, illustrates the big problem concerning the impartiality with this body, and is also inherent within other NPB dispute resolution mechanisms, including for doping disputes.

346. To further highlight this problem, the NPB commissioner (who is appointed by the clubs, with the players not able to participate in the appointment process) appoints the members of the Investigation Committee that adjudicate these salary arbitrations. The commissioner also adjudicates internal NPB disputes (including applying sanctions) based on lawsuits brought by the related parties. Consultation in connection with these disputes is carried out by the Investigation Committee.

347. In relation to doping disputes, these are adjudicated by the NPB Anti-Doping Investigation and Arbitration Committee, whose members are also selected by the commissioner. Moreover, complaints filed about this commission's decisions are dealt with by the NPB Anti-Doping Ad Hoc Committee, which again consists of members selected by the commissioner.

II. Football

348. In the J-League, as with the situation in professional baseball, problems with inadequate dispute resolution mechanisms have arisen. Basically, the J-League's chairman (who is appointed by the clubs, with the players not able to participate in the appointment process) adjudicates disputes involving contracts, transfers and sporting sanctions. Furthermore, it is the chairman who appoints the members of the consultative committee (named the Arbitration Committee). In practice, dispute resolution in the J-League is adjudicated by this chairman-appointed Arbitration Committee. Below are the details of the current system.

349. Generally, disputes in relation to contracts or transfers involving affiliated clubs or registered individuals under the auspices of the JFA (e.g., a dispute between

144. JEB Entertainment Co., Ltd. '10th Seminar on Supporting Players in the Football Business', from a DVD shown at the seminar in Tokyo on 12 Feb. 2011. Details of the DVD are available in Japanese at: http://www.jebentertainment.jp/news/20080526.html#semi10.

a player and his/her club concerning the club's unilateral termination of his contract) are to be resolved through a dispute resolution conciliation process analogous to mediation by the JFA Arbitration Committee (Article 6 of the JFA Conciliation Regulations) – one of the JFA's judicial organs, which is independent to the JFA Executive Committee.

350. The cost of applying for this conciliation process is JPY 100,000 (Article 9(3) of the JFA Conciliation Regulations). In order for a settlement from this process to take effect, all parties to the dispute must agree to the settlement or the judgment proposals formulated by the conciliators (Articles 17 and 18 of the JFA Conciliation Regulations). However, if no agreement can be reached on a settlement by the parties the conciliation process will break down (Article 20 of the JFA Conciliation Regulations). In other words, this dispute resolution process is not arbitration; it is merely a conciliation process.

351. Nevertheless, this conciliation process does not apply to disputes in the J-League (Article 6 of the JFA Conciliation Regulations) – a separate dispute resolution process is stipulated for the J-League. Basically, the J-League regulations state that regarding disputes in relation to contracts or transfers involving J-League clubs or players of the parties to the dispute pay a fee of JPY 100,000, they may apply for this dispute to be 'decided by the J-League chairman'. (Article 129 of the J-League Regulations and the J- League Arbitration Committee Regulations. Please note that the 'chairman' represents the J-League, and he is selected by the clubs; the players play no part at all in this selection.)

352. This is in effect an arbitration procedure, in which it is possible for the parties in dispute to agree upon a settlement (Article 15 and 16 of the J-League Arbitration Committee Regulations). However, this procedure differs from the JFA conciliation process in that if the parties in dispute do not agree on a settlement, the arbitration does not close and the chairman will decide the final outcome.

353. Furthermore, it is the chairman who appoints the members of the consultative committee (named the Arbitration Committee) with nobody from the players' side being involved in the committee at all. Therefore, it cannot be said in any way that the decisions handed down by this committee are administered by a fair, impartial third-party body. In other words, the disputes in the J-League (e.g., contract and transfer disputes) are dealt with by a so-called arbitration committee that cannot guarantee independence or impartiality.

354. To put it plainly, because the players cannot be involved in appointing the Arbitration Committee members, there are grave doubts over this body's ability to guarantee impartiality in the J-League's dispute resolution process. The Chairman's decision-making powers are enshrined of Article 157 of the J-League Regulations, which reads:

> In the J-League the decisions of the Chairman are final and binding in full on all related parties, individuals and organizations that belong to the J-League.

Accordingly, no objections or grievances whatsoever to the decisions of the Chairman can be brought by third parties to a court of law or other such related institutions.

355. In relation to contractual disputes, in the FIFA Circular no. 1129 (28 December 2007), FIFA obliges all its constituent associations to establish fair and impartial national dispute resolution chambers (NDRC). The members of these chambers should be composed of an equal number of player and club representatives to guarantee fair proceedings. However, it is obvious that the J-League's Arbitration Committee violates the provisions of this FIFA Circular. Accordingly, the JPFA is currently demanding that the JFA establish an NDRC in line with this FIFA circular.

356. In addition to the above, the *Ganaha Incident* highlights the major flaws concerning the impartiality of the J-League's dispute mechanism process. This is addressed in more detail below.

§6. Social Security

357. There is a nationwide system of public insurance schemes in operation. There are four types of public insurance:

(1) health insurance;
(2) pension insurance;
(3) industrial accident compensation insurance; and
(4) employment insurance.

358. Schemes (3) and (4) are only applicable to workers. Schemes (1) and (2) are split up into separate systems for workers and non-workers. In relation to scheme (1): the Employee Health Insurance system operates for employees, and the National Health Insurance system operates for all other parties. In relation to scheme (2): the National Employee Pension scheme operates for employees, and the National Basic Pension system operates for all other parties.

359. Let us consider the legal status of corporate sports players and professional sports players. The former, in relation to traditional amateur regulations, are usually contracted to the relevant corporations as employees and are, therefore, 'workers'. Conversely, the latter are not treated as 'workers' but as 'independent contractors'.

360. Therefore, it is common for professional sports players to enrol in schemes (1) and (2). However, they cannot participate in schemes (3) and (4). Please note that there is a partial exception for JSA sumo wrestlers who are enrolled in the National Employee Pension scheme.

§7. Tax Law

361. Sports players and coaches are obliged to pay income taxes. The Japanese tax code treats professional sports players not as 'workers' but as 'independent contractors'. Thus, their income is classified not as 'employment income' but as 'business income'. It is often the case that corporate sports players (semi-professional) are traditionally classified under amateur regulations as being employed as 'employees' of the said corporation with their income treated as 'employment income'. In the case of 'employment income', for the purpose of calculating income tax, estimated expenses are deducted as 'employment income deductions' (please note that for 'business income', this is calculated by deducting actual incurred expenses).

362. Income taxes are subject to withholding. Basically, the withholding tax system involves the payer of salary or remuneration making relevant deductions at source to pay taxes to the relevant parties. In other words, the sports player who is the recipient of the said salary or remuneration will receive the amount after withholding taxes are deducted.

363. The withholding tax system not only applies to residents (according to Article 2(1)(3) of the Income Tax Act (ITA), 'Residents are individuals who have their own residence in Japan or who have, up to now, a temporary residence in Japan continuously for over 1 year') but also to foreign players who are non-residents (according to Article 2(1)(4) of the ITA, 'Individuals who are not Resident').[145] Thus remuneration received by non-resident sports players who play for Japanese teams is classified as 'consideration received by a person who conducts a business that is mainly intended to provide personal services in Japan'. In general, the rate for withholding tax for non-residents is 20.42% of a player's income.

364. In order to reduce their tax burdens, it is commonplace for players to establish their own private companies. Revenue that is due to the personal skills of a player, such as prize money, must be reported to the tax authorities as individual earnings. Therefore, the commercial appearance fees and income from image rights form the core of revenues for these private companies.[146]

365. There are also certain schemes for tax exemption of revenues that athletes receive. For instance, the JOC, JPSA and those affiliated federations provide a tax-exempt cash reward for Olympic/Paralympic medal winners (Medallist Awards). Article 9 (1)(14) of the ITA provides that only the Medallist Awards are tax exempt and that similar awards from other sports associations are subject to taxation.[147]

145. *Income Tax Act*, law no. 33 of 1965 and amendment law no. 6 of 2007.

146. Okamoto, Katsuhide, *Issues in relation to the Taxation of Entertainment Corporations* 18 Natl. Tax C. Res. Papers 78 (1987).

147. Decision by Cabinet on 20 December 2019.

366. Sports players and coaches are also obliged to pay residential taxes (including prefectural and city residential taxes). Furthermore, as professional sports players are treated as independent contractors, they are obliged to pay individual enterprise tax. For players with an annual taxable sales income exceeding JPY 10 million, they will also be subject to the consumption tax.

367. Some sports contracts are subject to the payment of a special stamp tax. Contracts between athletes and clubs or sports associations in which athletes render services as professional baseball players, boxers, and wrestlers are subject to this taxation. The amount of stamp tax payable depends on the value of the athlete's contract, which is treated as a 'service contract' (Appendix 1(2) of the Stamp Tax Act and Article 21(1) of the Order for Enforcement of the Stamp Tax Act).[148, 149]

148. *Stamp Tax Act*, law no. 23 of 1967 and amendment law no. 26 of 2011.

149. *Order for Enforcement of the Stamp Tax Act*, ministerial order no. 108 of 1967 and ministerial order amendment no. 196 of 2008.

Part III. Doping and Sport

Chapter 1. General Issues

368. In 1964 at the Tokyo Olympics International Sports Committee meeting, a special doping panel was established, and in 1965, the first Doping Research Subcommittee was set up under the auspices of the JSPO Sports Medicine Research and Science Committee. Thereafter in 1985, the International Olympic Committee (IOC) approved the Mitsubishi Petrochemical Company Medical Science Corporation (now: Mitsubishi Chemical Medicine Corporation) as an authorized testing body,[150] which enabled full-scale doping tests to be carried out.

369. Following this, awareness of anti-doping became much stronger with incidents, such as the detection of eleven Chinese athletes with doping violations at the 1994 Twelfth Asian Games in Hiroshima and the suspension of a Japanese athlete in 1996 by an external testing body of the International Association of Athletics Federation. It was against this background that the JOC implemented its own anti-doping regulations in 1997, with JADA being formed in 2001, following the establishment of the World Anti-Doping Agency (WADA) in 1999.[151]

370. In fact, doping tests were introduced in 2003 by JSPO to the National Sports Festival. In December 2006, Japan became a signatory to UNESCO's 'International Convention against Doping in Sport',[152] and in May 2007, MEXT formulated and implemented its 'Guidelines for the Prevention of Doping in Sport'. Compliant with this trend, at present, many sports associations have joined JADA and the promotion of anti-doping activities continues apace.

371. Up until 2018, there had been no special statutory legislation in relation to doping in Japan, with anti-doping activities only taking the form of internal regulations within each sports association or organization. However, in view of the 2019 Rugby World Cup and the 2020 Tokyo Olympics, the Act on the Promotion of Anti-Doping Activities in Sport was enacted in June 2018, which entered into force on 1 October 2018. The Act on the Promotion of Anti-Doping Activities in Sport became

150. The Mitsubishi Chemical Medience Corporation's Doping Tests English website is available at: http://www.medience.co.jp/english/doping/index.html.
151. The WADA website is available at: http://www.wada-ama.org/.
152. The full text of the convention is available at: http://unesdoc.unesco.org/images/0014/001425/142594m.pdf#page=2.

the first domestic law to specify that doping practices were illegal, but the introduction of criminal penalties in the course of discussions on the enactment of the law was eventually postponed and no criminal penalties are imposed.

372. The use of substances prohibited by anti-doping regulations can also violate the Penal Code under legislation such as the Stimulants Control Act and the Cannabis Control Act,[153, 154] and thus be subject to corresponding criminal sanctions. Nevertheless, according to the principle of culpability in relation to Penal Code sanctions, parties cannot be punished regarding negligent or non-negligent consumption of such prohibited substances.

373. Although the associations of the major Olympic sports in Japan have joined JADA, there are doping-control cases carried out under the rules of professional sports organizations which are not JADA affiliated. This is particularly the case with professional baseball (please note that until 2009, the J-League also operated its own doping controls based on its independent doping rules).

374. There are two types of doping controls conducted in Japan, by:

(1) sports associations that are members of JADA and fully compliant with WADA's World Anti-Doping Code (WADA Code); and
(2) sports associations that are not members of JADA (e.g., independent) and which have not introduced the WADA Code.

These two types of doping controls shall be examined below.

153. *Stimulants Control Act*, law no. 252 of 1951 and amendment law no. 94 of 2006.
154. *Cannabis Control Act*, law no. 124 of 1948 and amendment law no. 160 of 1999.

Chapter 2. Public Regulation

375. JADA, which was established in 2001, carries out doping controls in full compliance with the WADA Code. Accordingly, JADA conforms with the definitions of *doping* as stipulated in the WADA Code (namely, 'Prohibited Substances and Methods'), along with the corresponding *doping sanctions* and the *due process* to be applied to these. Please note that generally for doping code violations, a four-year suspension is applied for first-time violations (Article 10.2.1 of the JADA Code).[155]

376. Under Article 13.2 of the JADA Code, doping violators have the right to appeal their decisions to either the CAS or the JSAA. These specific provisions are stated below:

– For appeals to the CAS, Article 13.2.1 reads:

> In cases arising from *Competition* in an *International Event* or in cases involving *International-Level Athletes*, the decision may be appealed exclusively to the *CAS* in accordance with the provisions applicable before such court.

– For appeals to JSAA, Article 13.2.2 reads:

> In cases involving *National-Level Athletes*, as defined by each National Anti-Doping Organization that do not have a right to appeal under Article 13.2.1, the decision may be appealed to the Japan Sports Arbitration Agency (JSAA).

155. The JADA Code is available in English and Japanese at: https://www.playtruejapan.org/upload_files/uploads/2018/04/jadacode2015v4_20180401.pdf.

Chapter 3. Private Regulation

377. In professional baseball, the definitions of *doping* are compliant with those stipulated in the WADA Code (namely, 'Prohibited Substances and Methods'). However, *doping sanctions* and the *due process* to be applied to these are administered through independent sports association regulations that do not conform to the WADA Code.

378. For instance, according to Article 2 of the NPB Anti-Doping Regulations which came into force in 2007, *doping* and *anti-doping rule violations* are defined as in the WADA Code. Furthermore, the same article stipulates that when the *anti-doping rules* and WADA Prohibited List are updated, the NPB regulations will automatically follow suit.

379. Article 10.3 of the NPB Anti-Doping Regulations stipulates the four sanctions below for doping violations, which differ from those in the WADA Code:

(1) Reprimand/warning (a written apology must be made and a warning is given about future conduct).
(2) Prescribed suspension (between one and ten official matches, inclusive).
(3) Prescribed suspension (one year or less of official matches).
(4) Indefinite suspension.

380. Up until now, there have been five cases in the NPB where violations of the anti-doping regulations have occurred. These cases are outlined below:

(1) *Case One:* In 2007, Rick Guttormson of the *Fukuoka Softbank Hawks* was suspended for twenty days after testing positive for *finasteride*, a hair growing agent that is illegal because it can be used as a masking agent. The player did not appeal the decision.[156]
(2) *Case Two*: In 2008, Luis Alberto González of the *Yomiuri Giants* was banned for one year after testing positive for the stimulants *clobenzorex* and *amphetamine*. The player appealed to the NPB Anti-Doping Ad Hoc Committee but this was rejected. González was released from his contract by the *Giants*.[157]
(3) *Case Three:* In 2008, Daniel Rios of the *Tokyo Yakult Swallows* was banned for one *year* after testing positive for *stanozolol*. The player appealed to the NPB Anti-Doping Ad Hoc Committee but this was rejected. Rios was released from his contract by the *Swallows*.[158]
(4) *Case Four:* In 2011, Hirokazu Ibata of the *Chunichi Dragons* was reprimanded after *testing* positive for *prednisolone*. Ibata used the banned substance to treat a chronic disease. Although he applied for a therapeutic use

156. NPB Anti-Doping Ad Hoc Committee Judgment, 10 Aug. 2007.
157. NPB Anti-Doping Ad Hoc Committee Judgment, 14 Jul. 2008.
158. NPB Anti-Doping Ad Hoc Committee Judgment, 2 Sep. 2008.

exemption (TUE) before, his failure to renew the TUE once the original exception period had expired led to his reprimand and a JPY 3 million fine on the club.[159]

(5) *Case Five:* In 2018, Japhet Amador of the Rakuten Golden Eagles was suspended for six months after testing positive for the banned substances chlortalidone and furosemide.[160]

(6) *Case Six:* In 2019, Joey Meneses of the Orix Baffaloes was suspended for one year after testing positive for the banned substances stanozolol.

(7) *Case Seven:* In 2019, Xavier Batista of the Hiroshima Carp was suspended for six months after testing positive for the banned substances clomifene and hydroxyclomifene.

381. Out of the first three cases, González and Rios appealed using attorneys as proxies to the NPB Anti-Doping Ad Hoc Committee. However, at the time, under the NPB Anti-Doping Regulations, the appeals body was specified as the same body that sanctioned the players, so there was very little expectation of the decisions being retracted. This illustrates the problem that, in practice, the appeals procedure was not guaranteed.

382. In relation to this problem, the NPB Anti-Doping Regulations underwent reforms in 2009. These provided for the establishment of a body at first instance, the 'Anti-Doping Inquest Tribunal' and an appeals body, the 'Anti-Doping Investigation and Arbitration Committee'. However, as the members of the 'Anti-Doping Ad Hoc Committee' are chosen by the NPB commissioner, there are grave doubts concerning the impartiality of this body (actually an appeal brought by Xavier Batista in 2019 was also rejected).

383. Furthermore, in relation to penalties, both the above players received one-year suspensions and subsequently fought against the validity of such decisions. Immediately prior to transferring to the NPB, González played in America and Rios in Korea. Nevertheless, the NPB sentences are considerably harsher when compared to those stipulated in the equivalent MLB and Korea Baseball Organization (KBO) anti-doping regulations. For instance, under the then-effective MLB regulations, the penalty for a first-time doping violation, such as using performance-enhancing steroids, was a fifty-match suspension (the equivalent of one-third of the season's games). Also, in these two countries, there were no punishments for the use of stimulants such as *ephedrine*. In fact, in the then-effective KBO, the penalty for a first-time doping offence was only a ten-game suspension (the equivalent of one-tenth of the season's games).

384. In professional football, the J-League was not a member of JADA in 2008 and operated its own non-WADA compliant anti-doping regulations. The *Ganaha Incident* (outlined in the 'Limits of the JSAA' section above) which occurred in 2007 was dealt with under this system. At the time *Kazuki Ganaha*, of the J-League

159. NPB Anti-Doping Ad Hoc Committee Judgment, 1 Sep. 2011.
160. NPB Anti-Doping Ad Hoc Committee Judgment, 9 Aug. 2018.

club *Kawasaki Frontale*, had a six-match suspension imposed on him by the league for an alleged violation of anti-doping regulations. This was imposed based on the sanctioning regime stipulated in the 'J-League Anti-Doping Regulations', not the WADA Code (please note that had *Ganaha* been sanctioned under the WADA Code, he would have, in principle, been subject to a two-year suspension). *Ganaha* eventually had his suspension overturned following his appeal to the CAS.[161]

385. In sumo wrestling, problems occurred when the wrestler *Wakanoho* was arrested in August 2008 for violating the Cannabis Control Act. Furthermore, immediately following this, in September, the positive cannabis tests of two wrestlers, *Roho* and *Hakurozan*, under urine tests administered by the JSA, led to massive calls for the need to introduce anti-doping regulations for sumo. However, at the time of writing, these had still not been introduced.

386. As a consequence of these events, the JSA terminated the employment of *Wakanoho*, *Roho*, and *Hakurozan*. Subsequent to this, the wrestlers challenged the terminations and brought their cases to the Tokyo District Court demanding recognition of their status as sumo wrestlers. However, the court dismissed each case.

387. The cases involving sumo wrestlers and cannabis do not end there because, in January 2009, *Wakakirin* was arrested for possessing the drug and subsequently suspended by the JSA.

161. *See* CAS Judgment, 26 May 2008.

Part IV. Sport and Commerce

Chapter 1. General Issues

§1. Introduction

388. The sports business can be viewed as a form of entertainment in which certain *rights* are traded, including broadcasting rights and official sponsorship rights. However, in Japan, there is no clear legal basis in statutory law upon which to regulate such rights. With other entertainment businesses, in cinema, for instance, *copyright* is substantiated through clear statutory law, and various types of business and contracts are administered based on this *copyright.*

389. Nevertheless, in the sports business, there are various intangible rights (for instance, *broadcasting rights*: the right to broadcast sports games live, in real-time) that are not afforded direct statutory protection. Therefore, these rights and their scope are characterized by their opacity.

390. Put another way, the sports business for a large part entails payment for the performance of a *contract*, the *value* of which is not directly protected by formal statutory rights. Business is also often carried out through the sale (e.g., by promoters such as clubs and sports associations) of this *value* in the form of *rights* which are determined by the internal regulations of these vendors. The terms for the sale of these *rights* are jointly decided by the vendors and the *rights* then become recognized through common business practice. Please note here that although sports business is also transacted based on formal statutory rights (such as the *trademarks* in team names and logos for merchandising, and *copyrights* in the sale of moving images of sports games), such cases tend to be very rare.

391. The revenues generated by sports broadcasting rights are massive. Although this is termed the *rights business*, the truth of the matter is that these rights do not even receive statutory protection as quasi-property rights (basically, there is no protection to claim injunctive relief against third parties). Therefore, another characteristic of the sports business is that it is based on *rights* which are comparatively weak.

392. The fragility of such rights is illustrated through so-called *ambush marketing* where parties that are non-official sponsors get a *free ride* in advertising their goods at sporting events. The same can also be said for parties that do not have broadcasting rights, which, during a game, can transmit that game in a separate format to the images from the stadium cameras.

393. Often rights in the sports business are formulated through the internal regulations of sports leagues and associations, and with many contractual relationships through various individual contracts based on these regulations. Therefore, these rights are in principle only effective within the parties to such contractual relationships and are not enforceable to third parties who are outside these relationships (in other words, these rights do not have a third-party effect).

394. Furthermore, it often occurs that the sports business *rights* in contracts are determined based on many contractual relationships between the parties that organize the matches (e.g., through league regulations). Thus, it is frequently the case that the content of these agreements is heavily weighted in the match organizers' favour and is also anti-competitive. As a result, there is a high risk that these agreements or contractual practices will face antitrust law issues such as a refusal to deal or an unreasonable restraint on trade. For instance, this situation is similar to those in America and Europe where antitrust issues have arisen for the bundling of broadcasting rights.

395. In terms of players' rights, there are also a great number of instances when these agreements or contractual practices unilaterally restrict such rights without the input or participation of the players. It goes without saying that the parties which strip the players of their rights face a massive risk of legal attack from the aggrieved parties (including, challenges by the players to the legal validity of such contracts).

396. The sports business represents various *partial societies* of autonomous sports associations (match organizers) that have created a plethora of internal rules, regulations, and structures. It is an established norm within these associations that the *rights* in the sports business are frequently determined through the said regulations, agreements, or contractual practices. There are many agreements and regulations in existence between these autonomous sports associations and parties extrinsic to these (e.g., different *partial societies*). For example, there are accords between amateur and professional sports associations, and the US-JPCA between the NPB and MLB.

397. In order to understand the legal issues in the sports business in Japan, it is necessary to grasp the substance and characteristics of this *source of law*. There is an examination below of the various legal issues in Japan's sports business.

§2. HOSTING AND PROMOTING EVENTS

I. Types of Events and the Legal Status of the Promotion Rights

398. Most of the fundamental revenue from hosting sports events (including golf, football, and professional baseball tournaments) is revenue derived from the place the event is promoted, such as admission fees, programme sales, merchandising and catering.

399. Basically, there are two methods of hosting events. The first involves staging events autonomously where the host bears the risks (autonomous promotion). The second involves selling promotion rights to promoters and agencies/distributors.

400. For specific sports matches in the case that the required participants, content, venue, and capital can be prepared, any party can host the matches. However, when hosting sports events that have a high entertainment value, it is necessary to promote the event with authorization from a respected sports organization.

401. In other words, the reason official football matches generate such value is because they are hosted with authorization from FIFA, JFA, or other authorities. In this way, it is considered that promotion rights are rights based on the official approval from these sporting organizations to promote games.

402. These promotion rights are not rights based on direct statutory grounds. However, take, for example, a party that despite not receiving official FIFA approval then hosts a football game that can be mistaken as having FIFA's approval. In this case, it is highly likely that this party will have violated statutory trademark rights and rights under the Unfair Competition Prevention Act (UCPA).[162]

403. Usually, such promotion rights are formulated through regulations such as the internal constitutions or rules of sports associations. For instance, when looking at professional sports in Japan, with baseball it is stipulated that the NPB will host the Nippon Series (Article 8(4) of the NPB Agreement and Article 3 of the Nippon Series Regulations). Also, in relation to the Pennant Race games (regular official games during the season), these are defined as home games in the regulations so the home team is regulated to host the game (Article 37 descending, of the NPB Agreement).

404. Please note that Article 165 of the NPB Agreement stipulates that the home team determines the entrance fee. Article 166 stipulates that the full revenue or majority of the revenue from the game shall be acquired by the home team (details are stipulated in each agreement of the Central League and the Pacific League).

---

162. *Unfair Competition Prevention Act*, law no. 47 of 1993 and amendment law no. 55 of 2006.

405. In relation to the J-League, the notions of 'host' (organizing a game in your own name) and 'supervise' (operating and executing a game at your own responsibility and expense) are distinct. In Article 44 of the J-League Regulations, it is stipulated that for all official games the J-League and JFA are 'hosts' and that the J-League is the 'supervisor'. The role of a 'supervisor' is then automatically delegated to each home team. Therefore, the practical risk involved in hosting official games is borne by the home team, as is the case with the Pennant Race games in baseball. In comparison, in the world of golf, organizations such as the Japan Golf Tour Organization and the Ladies Professional Golfers' Association of Japan just sanction the tournaments, while major sponsoring companies host the games. This means that the owners of the right to sanction the tournaments are different from the event promoters who actually host the tournaments.

406. The word 'host' is often used ambiguously. However, in this paper 'host' does not only bear the above meaning given in the J-League example (organizing a game in your own name), it also includes the meaning for 'supervise' (operating and executing a game at your own responsibility and expense).

II. Various Contracts Involved with Hosting and Promoting Events

407. Hosting and promoting events consists of three major elements: contents, venue, and money (capital).

A. Contracts Concerning Contents

408. To begin, promotion contents contracts are important in relation to defining the participants (teams and players) who will compete in the relevant games or event (tournament). These contracts shall be executed between the event promoter(s) and the participating athletes/players and their teams. If the competitors are individuals, these contracts shall be executed to register the athletes/players with the relevant sports associations or for entering tournaments (e.g., golf). These contracts (which include the pertinent regulations and matters to be observed and incorporate all necessary entry documentation) are executed after being signed.

409. In the case of team sports, such as baseball and football, contracts shall be executed between the players and the teams. There shall also be internal league regulations binding between the teams and individual contracts (including contracts for games against foreign teams).

B. Contracts Concerning Venues

410. Contracts in relation to venues are mainly leasing contracts for event organizers that do not possess suitable venues (e.g., stadiums). Recently the cases where the event organizers (including sports clubs) are commissioned to manage venues by the venue owners have been increasing. These include management permissions based on the Urban Park Act,[163] and the designated administrator system introduced based on the 2003 Local Autonomy Act reforms.

411. There are also contracts in relation to concession rights and revenue from merchandising (catering and fan items) in the stadiums.

C. Contracts Concerning Money (Capital)

412. There are two formats of contracts concerning capital in promoting events. The first format of contract is the sale of the rights connected with the promotion in part or whole to parties, including agencies or distributors. The second format of contract is the partnership by which the event promoters work collectively with various other companies (here, the event promoter's risks are borne in conjunction with the other companies).

413. Both formats of promotion are methods of capital fundraising. For instance, let us compare these formats with the methods of fundraising by movie productions. Here, the former style of promotion corresponds to the *pre-sales method*. The latter format of promotion corresponds to the *production partnership contract*. This is also called the *event executive committee method*. It is often the case here that the event host is labelled as 'XXX Executive Committee'. It is also common that parties such as advertising agencies, broadcasting stations, newspaper companies and promoters join as members of the executive committee.

414. In the first format of contract when part of the promotion rights is sold to outside parties, technically, the seller can retain the status of 'promoter' and the risks involved in the event. However, even the seller can sell all of the said rights where it does not bear any of the related risks.

415. For instance, the latter case is illustrated by the situation where a sports association (promoter) furnishes a company with a bundle of rights (including the sponsorship sales rights and broadcasting sales rights) for a sports event. Basically, for this, the association will receive a set amount of compensation in return, without bearing any of the risks of promoting the event.

416. On top of this, there is also a case where the sports association does not carry out the hosting itself of the match or tournament; it simply receives a set amount of money for selling the rights to the match or tournament (e.g., the association only receives money in the form of an endorsement fee).

163. *Urban Park Act*, law no. 79 of 1956.

D. Other Contracts in Connection with Hosting and Promoting Events (Promotion Revenue Contracts)

417. Other contracts for promoting events include: (a) contracts between the event host and the customers; and (b) contracts for outsourcing the ticket sales.

418. The types of contracts in (a) are often made in the form of adhesive terms and conditions, including consumers' waivers or unilateral contracts which are not exchanged in writing. In baseball, for instance, the NPB and its twelve clubs have published that their legal relations with the spectators are regulated through the: 'Match Viewing Contractual Terms & Conditions' and the 'Regulations Permitting Team Support'.

419. In relation to (b), outsourcing contracts allow the event host to wholly or partially outsource event day ticket sales operations to third parties.

Chapter 2. Public Regulation

§1. Media and Television Rights

I. Legal Scope and Limits of Broadcasting Rights

420. Sports events broadcasting rights revenues are at the core of the sports business. Even in Japan, broadcasting rights for the professional baseball team, the Yomiuri Giants, at the height of the team's popularity were sold for around JPY 100 million per game.

421. However, as aforementioned, many parts of the legal basis for *broadcasting rights* are unclear. Basically, sports matches are not copyrightable material under the Japanese copyright law, and it is not usual that an athlete's/player's performance is protected as a *performance* by neighbouring rights under the same law. Therefore, it is common that these broadcasting rights are not classified as intellectual property rights.

422. Accordingly, in Japan, it is recognized that broadcasting rights are based on acquiring consent from the facility (venue) owner/manager so the equipment for live transmission of the game can be brought to the venue. Therefore, in these cases, it is often explained that the rights of the grantors derive from the facility management of the venue.[164] (There is also a view that the broadcasting rights derive from an athlete's/player's image rights.)

423. It is frequently stipulated in the internal regulations of sports organizations which parties have the broadcasting rights for games and tournaments. For instance, in baseball, Article 44 of the NPB Agreement stipulates that the clubs hosting home games have the broadcasting rights for those games. In football, Article 119 of the J-League Regulations states that the broadcasting rights belong to the league itself.

424. There is an issue about whether the rights holders, such as broadcasting companies, can prohibit third parties from broadcasting or providing information in relation to the relevant games. In other words, if broadcasting rights means the rights to film games live with equipment in the stadium (which derives from the act of facility management), the issues stated below arise:

(a) Can the act of broadcasting a game from outside the stadium be prohibited?
(b) Can the act of providing game information except for the broadcast be prohibited?

425. In relation to issue *(a)*, let us consider an extreme but easy-to-understand example, such as an ultra-high performance camera, which is used to film and

164. *See* Part IV, Ch. 2, §3 'Merchandising' below.

broadcast the game from an aerial position a long way from the stadium. This cannot be classified as entering the stadium without authorization to film the game; thus the issue becomes whether such an act violates the facility management rights.

426. Even if this does not violate the real rights subsisting in facility management, as it is widely known that *broadcasting rights* in sports events are sold for a high price, it may be considered that these acts amount to rights violations and constitute illegal activity.

427. In relation to issue *(b)*, let us consider the problem where professional baseball games are transmitted almost ball for ball, real-time over the Internet. In Japan, there are no legal judgments on this problem. However, in America, the professional basketball league (National Basketball Association – NBA) brought and subsequently lost a case against the operators of *Sports Trax*, a mobile phone pager (similar to *PocketBell*) that transmitted live information about NBA games.[165]

428. This case serves as a reference to the lack of real rights for the act of providing information in connection with sports games. If such cases become a problem in Japan, it may be asserted that the acts of displaying indications of famous names/people are infringements of the UCPA. Nevertheless, it may be difficult to say in individual cases whether this conduct amounts to acts that create confusion with another person's goods or business.

II. Broadcasting Rights Contracts

429. It is commonplace for broadcasting rights contracts to be agreed between, on the one side parties that have the authority to bring into operation live broadcasts (as aforementioned this authority derives from unclear legal grounds as it is usually stipulated in internal sports association regulations) and on the other side broadcasting businesses (it is often the case that distributors, agencies, and agents also enter this contractual arrangement). On top of this, there are also cases where these broadcasting businesses act as a *licensor* when they re-grant their broadcasting rights to other parties.

430. A legal issue with broadcasting rights contracts concerns the copyright ownership of the broadcast images. Under general copyright law in Japan, live broadcast images do not fulfil the fixation requirements so it is difficult to say if these are protected as works by copyright law. Nevertheless, live transmissions that are simultaneously fixed as images can become cinematographic works, which may qualify for copyright protection. Please refer to the Tokyo High Court judgment of 25 September 1997, where it was recognized that in broadcasting a golf competition, the simultaneous recording of this onto a videotape was copyrightable as a cinematographic work.[166]

165. *The National Basketball Association v. Motorola, Inc.*, 105 F.3d 841 (2nd Cir. 1997).
166. Tokyo High Court Judgment, 25 Sep. 1997, Decision Times (*Hanrei Taimuzu*), vol. 994, 147.

431. Unless otherwise specified by contract, according to Article 29 of the Copyright Act, the owner of the copyright in a cinematographic work is the 'maker' who took the 'initiative and responsibility' for the work's production. Thus, it is considered that there are many cases where the broadcaster is the maker of the cinematographic work. In relation to this point, there are possibilities to stipulate in the contract that the copyright is owned by the event host/organizer (including relevant agencies), or the broadcaster (if this copyright is acquired in a consortium the members hold this in common), or that it is owned by both parties in common.

432. There are cases where the rights to the images of the tournament itself belong to the event's host but the copyright in the programmes using those images belong to the broadcasters. Or conversely, there are cases where it is assumed that the copyrights belong to the broadcasters but that the international images of the tournament are shared jointly between various parties.

433. In practice, even though these said copyrights are stipulated as being owned by the broadcasters, there are often contractual restrictions placed in relation to secondary use of the images (including, in producing DVDs of the event). Furthermore, whereas the broadcasters own the copyrights, there are occasions when the broadcasters are contractually obliged at the event host's request to provide the images free of charge.

III. Internet Broadcast Rights

434. The Internet broadcast of sports has become an important topic as a consequence of the rapid spread of smartphones and tablets. In the past, just like broadcasting rights, Internet rights were also owned and managed by broadcasting companies. Recently, however, Internet rights are increasingly treated differently than broadcasting rights, and there has been a trend for sporting event organizers to regain their rights. For instance, J-League entered into a ten-year, EUR 1.85 billion deal with DAZN, a sports streaming service provided by the major British Internet company of Perform Group. This deal dwarfs the JPY 5 billion-per-annum long-term broadcasting deal between J-League and Sky PerfecTV, a major Japanese satellite broadcaster (The average annual amount of the DAZN deal is approximately EUR 185 million, about four times the size of the Sky PerfecTV contract). What is more, this amount is only the minimum guarantee. If a certain level of revenue is reached, DAZN will share the additional revenue with J-League. With this contract, J-League switched to a policy of producing game footage in-house and owning the copyright of the footage (J-League explains that this is the first time that a major football league in the world has entered into a contract with an Internet company in the market of paid broadcasting.).

§2. SPONSORING

I. Legal Basis and Limits of Sponsorship Rights

435. It goes without saying that sponsorship revenue is a major revenue source for the sports business.

436. *Sponsorship rights* are not protected by formal statutory law. However, there are cases when non-official event sponsors use an event's official mark in advertising so as to create confusion with the event's official sponsor. In such cases, these non-official sponsors are likely to have violated corresponding trademark rights and rights under the UCPA.

437. Even despite the existence of official sponsors with sponsorship rights, rival companies that do not possess such rights, without using the official event mark, have developed a broad range of advertising activities that are akin to the rights of these official sponsors. For instance, when the FIFA World Cup is held, there is much advertising that uses football images with slogans such as 'We support Japan'. This is known as the *ambush marketing* problem.

438. With ambush marketing, if it is executed well without using the official event mark, it is then very difficult to utilize trademark rights and rights under the UCPA to prevent such marketing. When considering pursuing legal responsibility under the widely interpreted UCPA concepts of 'using an indication of goods or business' and 'confusion'. There are many difficult points that arise.

439. Even when trademark rights exist, such as with the FIFA World Cup, there is a danger that through the generalization of the 'Football World Cup' name, the mark perhaps loses its distinctive commercial appeal, and therefore its effectiveness. In order to avoid this undesirable situation FIFA demands that various types of media in relation to describing the World Cup must do so by affixing the '™' sign to FIFA's slogans as such: 'FIFA World Cup™'.

II. Players' Image Rights and Endorsement Contracts

440. There are many cases where individual athletes are also sponsored by companies as well as the aforementioned clubs, leagues, and sports associations. This type of corporate sponsorship often takes the form of endorsement contracts (contracts pertaining to using the athlete's distinctiveness and features to endorse and advertise products).

441. The legal basis for this type of business is publicity rights as a form of image rights. In Japan image rights are construed in two ways, privacy rights and publicity rights. Images that are for commercial use, such as sponsorship and endorsements, fall under the latter category of publicity rights.

442. Image rights in Japan, both privacy rights and publicity rights, are not prescribed under formal statutory law but are rights established through judicial precedent. Therefore, the scope of image rights differs from statutory intellectual property rights (e.g., trademarks and copyrights) with large parts of the former remaining imprecise even today. Nevertheless, at the very least, there is no doubt that the scope of publicity rights extends to the use of players' images in advertising. This is addressed in more detail below in the 'The Legal Basis for Use of the Images of Players and Athletes in the Merchandizing Business' section.

443. Sponsorship and endorsement contracts for athletes and sports stars involve such parties performing not only in advertising for the supporting companies but also in displaying the sponsors' names on uniforms and related sporting equipment. Some endorsements may also take the form of sports goods manufacturers providing relevant goods to the athletes.

444. There are also cases where individual sports like golf, track and field, and swimming are sponsored by companies through the way of 'belonging' to these companies. In such cases, the corporate name will be announced every time the player participates in a tournament, so it is expected that this advertising will have a big effect.

445. In relation to amateur sports athletes, entering into such contracts is often in itself prohibited or can lead to the loss of an athlete's amateur status.

§3. MERCHANDISING

I. Legal Basis for Merchandising Rights

446. Sports merchandising revenue (sports licensing), which is based on the use of branding (popularity and attracting customers) as intangible property connected with sport is also a mainstay of the sports business. Sports branding can be generally classified as such:

(1) brands of sports organizations including clubs and leagues (e.g., Hanshin Tigers and the J-League);
(2) brands for sports events (e.g., the Olympics and the FIFA World Cup); and
(3) brands for athletes and sports players.

447. First, the legal basis for merchandising rights is substantiated through the registration of the brand's features (e.g., name and logo) as trademark rights. Legally speaking, approval for merchandising is provided through licensing the use of such trademarks.

448. Second, even when there is no trademark registration, it is often the case that famous team names and logos are protected under Article 2(1)(i) and (ii) of the UCPA (which cover acts of displaying indications of famous names and people).

Therefore, when unregistered famous team names and logos are used in merchandising without permission by unlicensed third parties, such conduct could infringe the UCPA.

449. In relation to this point, there is a significant Japan Supreme Court judgment (29 May 1984) on the so-called *American Football Incident.*[167] In this case, a seller of self-assembly box lockers that were emblazoned in a houndstooth check style with the team marks of seven American NFL teams was sued by NFL Properties (NFLP, the NFL's rights management company) and Sony Corporation (the master licensee for NFL products in Japan), which sought an injunction preventing these sales as an infringement of the former UCPA. The Supreme Court concluded that the act of the seller constituted an infringement of the former UCPA. This is because the seller's acts in using an indication of goods or business that were identical or similar to the merchandising group's (group: NFLP, Sony Corporation and its licensees) goods and business could create confusion among consumers that the seller belonged to this group.

450. Accordingly, caution is required, as the use of famous team names and logos in merchandise can potentially give rise to UCPA violations, by creating confusion as to the existence of a licensor-licensee relationship.

451. Please note, however, that the rather wide interpretation applied in the aforesaid judgment makes it difficult to say whether the use of an 'indication of goods' in itself can constitute an act which creates confusion as to the relationship of licensor-licensee. Therefore, caution is required when deducing that only using 'an indication of goods' cannot be an infringement of the UCPA.

452. In relation to the mark of the IOC, the manner of use of an identical or similar mark as a trademark that is likely to mislead the public as to the existence of a relationship with the IOC is regulated by UCPA Article 17 and specific ordinances thereunder. In the same manner, prohibitions on the commercial use of other marks and emblems that are specified by Japanese government ordinances is regulated by Articles 16(1), 16(3) and 17 of the UCPA (these articles cover the use of: foreign national flags, emblems and crests; seals and signs of a foreign State or local government for supervision or certification purposes; and marks that represent international organizations).

453. There are also cases where team symbols, including mascot characters, can receive protection under copyright law. Design right issues also arise when other items such as team uniforms are registered as designs.

454. As shall be addressed below, athletes' merchandising rights are substantiated legally through publicity rights, a type of image right. However, because these

167. Supreme Court of Japan Judgment, 29 May 1984, Civil Decisions Reporter (*Minshu*), vol. 38, no. 7, 920 and Decision Times (*Hanrei Taimuzu*), vol. 530, 97.

publicity rights do not extend to the use of names of things (e.g., tangible things), it is impossible to assert such rights legally for the use of names and logos of famous teams.[168]

455. There has even been a trademark case concerning a famous baseball team name, where an individual not connected with the Hanshin Tigers baseball team registered the *Hanshin Yusho* (English translation: *Hanshin Champions*) trademark. Please note, once it was recognized that the trademark was fully registered in 2004, in the following year, Hanshin Tigers were successful in a legal claim to invalidate the said trademark.

456. In another case, the trademark owner of the name *Juventus*, a professional Italian football team, brought an injunction action against an import seller of official *Juventus* goods demanding the prevention of these import sales. The court held that this type of action constituted an abuse by the trademark owner of his rights thereunder.[169] There was also an invalidation action brought against the trademark. However, at the time of trademark application, *Juventus* was not a famous or well-known name in Japan and was not likely to cause damage to public policy under Article 4(1)(7) of the Trademark Act, thus the action failed.[170]

II. Legal Basis for Use of the Images of Players and Athletes in the Merchandising Business

457. Image rights (publicity rights) form the legal basis for the use of players' and athletes' images in brand merchandising.

458. Publicity rights are not rights which are substantiated under formal statutory law but rights which have been established through judicial precedent. Therefore, even today the scope of publicity rights, which is different to that of copyrights and trademarks, is unclear. It is no doubt that advertising which uses a player's image is within the scope of publicity rights. However, there is a case where the use of a famous player as a topic of a book was denied as a violation of his publicity rights.[171] Thus, there are situations where the scope of players' image rights (publicity rights) can and cannot extend to the use of players' images in merchandising goods.

459. When deciding whether the publicity rights have been infringed or not, recent cases have based their decisions on whether the alleged infringement is mainly intended to use the unique ability of the images to attract customers.[172]

168. Supreme Court of Japan Judgment, 13 Feb. 2004, Civil Decisions Reporter (*Minshu*), vol. 58, no. 2, 311 and Decision Times (*Hanrei Taimuzu*), vol. 1156, 101.
169. Tokyo District Court Judgment, 23 Mar. 2000, Decision Times (*Hanrei Taimuzu*), vol. 1035, 234.
170. Tokyo High Court Judgment, 24 Mar. 1999, Decision Times (*Hanrei Taimuzu*), vol. 1683, 138.
171. Tokyo District Court Judgment, 29 Feb. 2000, Decision Times (*Hanrei Taimuzu*), vol. 1028, 232.
172. Supreme Court of Japan Judgment, 2 Feb. 2012, Supreme Court Civil Case Reporters, Vol. 66, no. 2, p. 89.

According to these judgments, the main determining factor is the effect that the selling power of the player's image has on the value of the corresponding goods. Thus, when the proportion of factors outside the selling power of a player's image (e.g., the effect of original work and effort of the goods creator) in the goods is small, such goods which use a player's image for merchandising will fall within the scope of the player's publicity rights and violate those rights accordingly.

460. In the *Sadaharu Oh Medal Incident*, the Tokyo District Court held that using a professional baseball player's image in unauthorized merchandising violated that player's image rights.[173]

§4. Ownership of Clubs

461. Since the Japanese economic bubble burst, the corporate sports system has been in the decline, with many corporate sports clubs going out of existence altogether. In particular, between 1998 and 2002, the situation became very critical with clubs disappearing at a rate of over thirty per year.[174] Once corporations realized the limitations of the model for operating sports clubs essentially as a vehicle for advertising themselves, the process of these clubs developing independently took hold. Sports clubs went from the model of being owned by specific corporations to a model of being run as independent clubs. To cover their operating costs, such clubs became reliant on contributions from small sponsors and supporter groups.

462. As baseball, football, and basketball became professionalized, the ownership of the clubs in these clubs transferred from corporations whose main business is unrelated to sports to independent legal entities which were established for the specific purpose of owning the clubs. Many of the clubs have eliminated the names of their former corporate owners from the clubs' names and adopted the names of the cities where their home stadia are based. By adopting this region-focused approach, professionalized sports have been able to achieve success in attracting a loyal fan base.

173. Tokyo District Court Judgment, 2 Oct. 1978, Decision Times (*Hanrei Taimuzu*), vol. 372, 97.
174. Sasakawa Sports Foundation, *The 2006 SSF White Book on Sports* 101 (Sasakawa Sports Foundation 2006).

Chapter 3. Competition Law

§1. Sports and the Application of Competition Law

463. In sports in Japan, up until the present day, there have been very few issues involving competition law (in Japan, the main competition law statute is the 'Act on Prohibition of Private Monopolization and Maintenance of Fair Trade').[175] However, just merely by looking at the various restrictive trade practices in sport, it is considered that there should be rather more applications of competition law.

464. For instance, historically in America, there are often restrictions on the freedom of players to transfer, which are infringements of competition law. Thus, from the point when Japan adopted the American model of professional baseball, with its accompanying restrictive trade practices, vigorous debate has long ensued about whether these practices infringe the Anti-Monopoly Act.

465. The aforementioned 1978 *Egawa Incident* is an example of when the restrictive trade practices in professional Japanese baseball were questioned from a competition law perspective. At the time this incident prompted heated discussion in the Japanese parliament about whether the draft system constituted an unfair restraint to trade (e.g., a cartel) under Article 2(6) of the Anti-Monopoly Act. In subsequent questioning of the JFTC Secretary General by the Upper House Legal Committee, he answered that players' contracts were employment contracts and the equivalent thereto. He also stated to the effect that the Anti-Monopoly Act did not apply to such employment contracts. Moreover, JFTC did not mention any of its rationale behind this type of interpretation.[176]

466. On the other hand, twenty-six years later in 2004, competition law violation issues surfaced again during the baseball reorganization problem (please note, the baseball reorganization problem is also referred to in paragraphs 15–17). This time the debate concerned whether massive entry fees demanded by the NPB for new entrants to the league constituted a violation of the Anti-Monopoly Act.

467. On 4 August 2004, in an Upper House Education Policy Committee meeting, the JFTC stated that an examination into the reasonableness of these entry fees should be undertaken. The JFTC also asserted that in general, it would take considerable interest in relation to the issue of new teams being barred entry to the league without due cause.[177] Therefore, debate took hold on the premise that competition law is applicable to the NPB entry fee system.

468. Following this, in a separate issue, professional baseball players sued the clubs, claiming that the clubs' comprehensive management of their image rights

175. As aforementioned in para. 315, this Act is referred in this paper to as the 'Anti-Monopoly Act'.
176. Masato Dougauchi & Yoshihisa Hayakawa (eds), *An Introduction to Sports Law* 265 (Kyoto: Minerva Shobou Ltd., April 2011).
177. *Ibid.*, 257.

based on the NPB Uniform Player Contract infringed the Anti-Monopoly Act. It was affirmed by each court during this long-running legal battle that competition law should apply in relation to matters concerned with the uniform contract.[178]

469. For the professional baseball clubs as *operators* of the sports business, it is obvious that their conduct in the above examples is subject to the rules of competition law. There is no statute or legal judgment in Japan to exempt the application of competition law. In relation to this point, it was previously mentioned that at the very least professional baseball players are treated as 'workers' under the LUA. The issue then becomes whether the Anti-Monopoly Act is applicable to the employment relations between the players and clubs under the players' contracts. In line with the judgments from the above image rights cases, the courts did not reject that competition law could be applied to the treatment of image rights based on these contracts.

470. Even when considering the view that competition law does not apply to an employment relationship, it has been asserted that it is a separate issue as to whether the reserve and draft systems unfairly restrict competition. This is in the sense that, these systems operate to place restrictions on the players' freedom to execute contracts in a 'field of business' where the players are 'suppliers' and the clubs are 'users', under Article 2(4)(2) of the Anti-Monopoly Act.

471. Accordingly, it is often asserted that there are no impediments to the application of competition law in sports. Henceforth, as in America, when the players' awareness of this matter heightens there is likely to be a corresponding increase in the legal debate on the application of competition law in Japan. In fact, JFTC in its report on 'Human Resource and Competition Policy' which was published on 15 February 2018,[179] says that, 'For instance, if restriction of transferring or switching is jointly determined with the purpose of maintaining or improving the level of services provided by a professional sports league consisting of a number of teams, such circumstances are considered in assessing the legality of such conduct under the Anti-Monopoly Act.' This means that those anti-competitive practices can be a violation of the Anti-Monopoly Act. It is against this background that JFTC, after 2018, launched investigations, as aforementioned, into the transfer restrictions on corporate sports athletes (e.g., amateur athletics), the NPB's so-called *Tazawa Rule* and the JBC's transfer restrictions on boxers in terms of possible violations of antitrust laws and all of them have been abolished as a consequence.

472. Below there is an examination of the various systems employed in professional baseball that concern issues of competition law.

178. *See* Tokyo District Court Judgment, 1 Aug. 2006; Tokyo High Court Judgment, 25 Feb. 2008; and Supreme Court of Japan Judgment, 6 Jun. 2010.

179. https://www.jftc.go.jp/en/pressreleases/yearly-2018/February/180215_files/180215_2.pdf.

§2. PROFESSIONAL BASEBALL DRAFT SYSTEM AND RESERVE SYSTEM UNDER COMPETITION LAW

473. It has long been pointed out that the draft and reserve systems in professional baseball, which restrict players' freedom to execute contracts, constitute infringements of the Anti-Monopoly Act.

474. In particular, it is asserted by legal commentators that first, the agreements between all twelve NPB clubs represent an 'unfair restraint of trade' under Article 3. Second, the actions of the NPB, as the trade association (Article 8 of the Anti-Monopoly Act) of the twelve clubs, substantially restricts competition.[180]

§3. RESTRICTIONS CONCERNING THE ENTRY OF NEW TEAMS TO THE NPB AND COMPETITION LAW

475. In 2004, two professional baseball clubs, *Osaka Kintetsu Buffaloes* (*Kintetsu*), then owned by Kintetsu Corporation, and the *Orix Blue Wave* (*Orix*), a team in the same league, surprised the whole of Japan when they announced their merger.

476. The *Kintetsu-Orix* merger, which reduced the number of baseball teams in the twelve-team professional league (run on a two-league format with six teams in each league), acted as a trigger for powerful club owners and the NPB to reorganize the leagues further. This plan to reorganize the professional baseball world became a big issue when the owners expressed their intention to merge two other clubs into one, and thereby restart the professional league on a ten-team, one-league format.

477. The determined opposition to these reorganization plans went as far as the JPBPA holding a strike (please note the strike was held for two days on 18 and 19 September 2004). In the end, facing a barrage of opposition from the JPBPA and public opinion, the owners backed down and maintained the twelve-team two-league format. *Rakuten* subsequently replaced *Kintetsu*, which withdrew from the league.

478. During this process of team reorganization, it was even debated in the Japanese parliament whether the internal NPB regulations that stipulated conditions for the entry of new teams to the NPB were in violation of the Anti-Monopoly Act. Namely, in accordance with NPB regulations at that time for a new team to enter the NPB, this team had to pay an affiliation fee of JPY 6 billion (for taking over an existing team by entering the league the fee is JPY 3 billion).

479. It was widely felt that the imposition and collection of such outrageously high fees were illogical based on social convention. Moreover, as such fees unreasonably restricted the entry of members into a trade association, it was also believed

180. Takayasu Okushima, *Nippon Professional Baseball Agreement and Antitrust Law*, 1993(1032) Jurist 29 (Yuhikaku Publishing Co., Ltd., 1993).

to have violated Article 8 of the Anti-Monopoly Act (please also refer to the JFTC 'Guidelines Concerning the Activities of Trade Associations under the Anti-Monopoly Act').[181]

480. The JFTC delivered an opinion on this requiring the NPB to indicate on what basis the JPY 6 billion fees were reasonable. In response, the NPB reformed its system regarding the entry of new teams. These reforms stipulated that for new teams to enter the NPB they have to pay an entry fee of JPY 500 million (in accordance with Article 36(7) and (8) of the NPB Agreement), this fee comprised JPY 100 million as an enrolment fee and JPY 400 million for the 'Baseball Promotion Fund' and JPY 2.5 billion as a security deposit (in accordance with Article 36(5) of the NPB Agreement, this security deposit would be returned after ten years). These developments, naturally, were of great assistance to *Rakuten* in its entry to the NPB.

§4. Issues Concerning Professional Baseball Players' Image Rights and Competition Law

481. As aforementioned, the professional baseball players in Japan sued the NPB clubs over the management of the players' image rights. The players claimed that as they were themselves denied from managing these rights, this constituted a violation of the Anti-Monopoly Act. To be more precise, the players cited three instances of unfair trade practices under the Anti-Monopoly Act employed by the NPB clubs, namely:

(1) abuse of a Dominant Position (Article 2(9)(5));
(2) trading on Restrictive Terms (Article 2(9)(4)); and
(3) concerted Refusal to Trade (Article 2(9)(1)).

482. In the end, these unfair trade practice claims were not admitted. However, this spate of image rights litigation was prompted by a prior case where the NPB's management of such rights raised another Anti-Monopoly Act violation issue. In 2000, the NPB granted Konami Corporation the exclusive right to exploit the players' image rights in the professional baseball computer game for a period of three years. From this, it transpired that other computer-game publishers could not use the players' images in their baseball games without Konami's consent.

483. As part of this exclusive agreement, Konami had originally agreed to grant sub-licences to other computer-game developers. However, as a result of Konami's

181. JFTC, *Guidelines Concerning the Activities of Trade Associations under the Antimonopoly Act* (JFTC 1995), these are available in English at: https://www.jftc.go.jp/en/legislation_gls/imonopoly_guidelines_files/tradeassociation.pdf.

conduct in unfairly delaying the conclusion of these sub-licences with certain developers, on 22 April 2003, the JFTC officially warned Konami that its conduct was in danger of violating the Anti-Monopoly Act (please note the NPB also received a caution).[182]

§5. Antitrust Issues Relating to Consumption Tax on Pro-baseball Player Compensation

484. In Japan, professional baseball players have the obligation to pay the consumption tax on their salary. The salary of professional baseball players had been shown as the after-tax price for a long time. When a consumption tax of 3% was introduced in 1989 and an increase to 5% was introduced in 1997, controversies arose because some teams failed to increase the players' compensation in proportion to the increase in the consumption tax. Since the total tax-included amounts remained unchanged, the players' salary in substance decreased by the amount of the consumption tax (The 'rejection of consumption tax pass-down problem').

485. Article 2(9)(v) (General Designation Article 14) of the Anti-monopoly Act prohibits enterprises from using their superior bargaining position to refuse to add the increased consumption tax to the total purchase prices (Guidelines on the Consumption Tax Pass-down and the Anti-Monopoly Act). Therefore, the pro-baseball teams' refusal to carry the consumption tax of players' compensation could be considered a violation of the Anti-Monopoly Act.

486. The *Act on Special Measures on Correcting the Obstruction of Passing Down to Ensure Smooth and Proper Consumption Tax Pass-Downs* (Act on Special Measures of Pass-Downs) was enacted in response to the increase of the consumption tax from 5% to 8% in 2014. Article 3.1 of the Act on Special Measures of Pass-Downs prohibits parties from 'driving a hard bargain' to refuse the pass-down of the consumption tax. Consequently, teams' refusal to bear the pass-down of the consumption tax is now also deemed an illegal bard bargain that is prohibited by the Anti-Monopoly Act.

§6. Other Issues

487. In boxing, there were cases where the establishment of new gyms involved Anti-Monopoly Act violation issues, and thus prompted a JFTC investigation in 1993. Basically, in order to open a boxing gym in Japan, it is necessary to apply for a licence with the Japan Boxing Commission. Furthermore, to acquire the licence, it was a requirement that the applicant becomes a member of the Japan Boxing Association (JBA). At the time of the investigation in 1993, Article 2(3) of the association's entry regulations stipulated that membership was dependent upon securing the approval of the three nearest members in the same regional boxing association.

182. *See* para. 359.

488. In light of this, following its investigation, the JFTC cautioned the JBA that such conduct could violate Article 8(1)(4) of the Anti-Monopoly Act on 1 March 1993, which prevents trade associations from limiting the number of entrepreneurs in a field of business. The JBA responded by voluntarily scrapping the offending regulations.

Chapter 4. COVID-19 and Its Impact on National Sports

§1. Impact

489. The effects of COVID-19 began to emerge in late February 2020. First, the interruption of professional football (J-League), which had begun on 21 February was decided on 25 February. Then on 9 March, it was decided that the opening of professional baseball scheduled on 20 March would be postponed indefinitely. On 23 March, the season of the Rugby Top League, which was scheduled to continue until 9 May, was discontinued. On 24 March, the Tokyo Olympic and Paralympic Games were postponed for one year. On 27 March, the season of the professional basketball B.League, which was scheduled to continue until 9 May, was discontinued. On 26 April, the All Japan High School Athletic Tournament (Inter High) was cancelled. On 20 May, the All Japan High School Baseball Summer Tournament (so-called Koshien), the largest event in the amateur baseball world, was also cancelled.

490. In June, there was a gradual movement toward the resumption of sporting events. On 19 June, the professional baseball season started about three months later, and on July 4, professional football J-League resumed. At this point, only matches without spectators were allowed. However, from 10 July, spectators were permitted in a limited number. However, it was mandatory for the audience to wear a mask, and they are prohibited from cheering.

§2. Measures

491. In addition to the generally applicable support measures (e.g., emergency loans), the government also provided special measures to the sports industry. Such measures can be roughly divided into the following:

(A) Subsidies for operational support (related to infection prevention measures associated with the holding of matches, expenditures for responding to changes in spectator admissions, and cancellation costs incurred in accordance with the declaration of a state of emergency).
(B) Tax reform. For example, it was clarified that a profit-making enterprise, which is an owner or sponsor of a professional sports club, would be allowed to deduct various expenses used for the club (such as loss compensation and waiver of the right to claim reimbursement of sponsorship fees). It is also clarified that any loans provided by such enterprises to clubs at low-interest rates or without interest would not be regarded as donations under tax law. In addition, measures were introduced to reduce the tax burden on fans by making the ticket price eligible for a charitable deduction if the fans voluntarily abandon ticket refund claims for matches cancelled due to the influence of COVID-19.
(C) Subsidies to individual athletes and small- and medium-sized sports organizations for measures to continue sporting activities (such as the creation of a new training environment and development of an online environment).

492. As for professional sports, professional baseball and football, Japan's two largest professional sports, have been holding joint meetings on COVID-19 countermeasures to discuss the establishment and revision of protocols for the safe operation of games on an ongoing basis since March 2020.

493. As for professional baseball, the number of games was reduced from 143 games to 120 games (down about 16%) due to a delayed opening of three months and the limitation on the number of spectators. However, the salaries of the players were not reduced.

494. As for J-League Football, the total number of games played in the season (J1-34 games) was not reduced despite the approximately three-month interruption of the season. Like professional baseball, there was a limitation on the number of spectators, but the salaries of the players were also not reduced. In the 2020 season, relegations to lower divisions were also suspended.

495. Both the basketball B.League and the rugby Top League ended their season early in March 2020, but the salaries of athletes were not reduced.

Chapter 5. Tokyo 2020 Olympics and Paralympics

§1. 'Unity in Diversity' and Human Rights

496. The Tokyo 2020 Games were the first ones in the history of the Olympic and Paralympic Games to be postponed by a year. It was also the first time the Olympic Games expressly declared that they would be held in accordance with the UN Guiding Principles on Business and Human Rights, based on the concept of 'Unity in Diversity'. The Games drew attention to various human rights initiatives and issues.

497. First, Tokyo 2020 was the first Olympics with the participation of a transgender athlete (Laurel Hubbard from New Zealand) based on the guidelines published by the IOC in 2015. Although such participation was controversial in terms of human rights and competition fairness, no legal disputes arose. On the other hand, amidst ongoing litigation in the European Court of Human Rights over the prohibition by the World Athletics of Caster Semenya, a two-time medallist of 800 meters in past Olympic Games, two Namibian female athletes were banned from participating in the 400-meter race due to their high testosterone levels (though they were allowed to participate in the 200-meter races). The Tokyo Games demonstrated the effects of the regulations implemented by the World Athletics in 2019 (these regulations also affected the qualifications of DSD athletes from Africa, such as Kenya, Burundi and Niger, to participate in the Olympic Games).

498. In addition, from the viewpoint of Athlete Activism which has gained momentum due to the Black Lives Matter Movement, heated debates took place over whether Rule 50.2 of the Olympic Charter violates athletes' freedom of expression because this rule restricts protest activities at competition venues. In this regard, in December 2020, more than half a year before the Olympic Games, the USOPC made it clear that it would not impose sanctions on peaceful protests against racial discrimination that did not constitute a divisive disruption. Therefore, attention was paid to whether or not the IOC has moved toward the relaxation of Rule 50.2. On 2 July 2021, immediately before the Olympic Games, the IOC announced Rule 50.2 Guidelines and clarified the relaxation of the application of the Rules by, for example, allowing protests to take place even in the venues prior to the competitions. As a result, peaceful protests such as kneeling at the beginning of the football tournament were conducted successfully, and there were no cases where sanctions were imposed under Rule 50.2 during the tournament.

499. On the other hand, there was the incident of Belarussian sprinter Krystsina Tsimanouskaya, who had been engaged in activities such as posting critical comments about the Belarussian government and urging the government to guarantee freedom of speech before the Olympics. In response to a social media post by her on 30 July 2021 criticizing the inadequacy of the Belarus Olympic Committee, it ordered her to return to Belarus during the Olympic Games and she was forcibly taken to Haneda Airport on 1 August 2021. At the airport, she sought protection from the Japanese police. In the end, the athlete sought asylum in Poland without being able to participate in the 200-meter race, which was scheduled for the next day. On 2 August, Ms Tsimanouskaya made an Urgent Application for the Stay of the Appealed Decision to the ad hoc division of the CAS to reverse the Belarusian NOC's decision banning her from participating in the 200-meter race (CAS OG 20/13; the motion was dismissed on the following day).[183]

Just before the opening of the Paralympic Games, the Taliban took control of the regime in Afghanistan. Two athletes from Afghanistan, whose participation in the Games became doubtful, arrived in Tokyo on 28 August with the help of the Australian government and other agencies, and were able to participate in the competition on 29 August and later. This has resulted in an event of interest in the aspects of human rights infringement and rescue.

500. Regarding human rights over the Tokyo Olympic and Paralympic Games, a grievance mechanism was introduced to receive disputes over the Tokyo 2020 Sustainable Sourcing Code, including human rights violations in the procurement process, which were stipulated from the perspective of sustainable procurement at the preparatory stage of the Olympic and Paralympic Games. By September 2021, sixteen claims had been filed.[184]

§2. COVID-19 – Laws and the 'Playbook'

501. Since Tokyo 2020 was held in an unprecedented pandemic, it was strictly restricted by various laws and regulations in order to make it a safe event with infection control measures. Problems from the viewpoint of the legal rights of athletes and other parties involved in the tournament became a focal point.

502. Relevant regulations were imposed by the Government of Japan as well as organizers of the Games, including the IOC, the International Paralympic Committee (IPC), and the Tokyo 2020 Olympics and Paralympics Organizing Committee (TOCOG). The regulations implemented by the Government of Japan mainly relate to border measures and quarantine measures. In relation to this, Special Measures for Athletes and Officials for the Tokyo Games for the entry to and departure from Japan were established. Regarding special measures, the following criticisms were heard: the issue of fairness among the participating countries caused by differences in infection conditions in each country (e.g., strict regulations were imposed on India, where the delta strain of COVID-19 was prevalent); and the lack of special measures for the families of athletes made it difficult for athletes with infants requiring breastfeeding to participate in the tournament.

503. The measures by the IOC, the IPC and TOCOG were published in a Playbook.[185] The insufficiency of measures against infection and the legality of forcing players to agree to waive certain rights were also criticized. In May 2021, TOCOG

183. https://www.tas-cas.org/fileadmin/user_upload/OG_20-13_Order_for_publication.pdf.
184. https://olympics.com/tokyo-2020/en/games/sustainability/sus-code#01.
185. https://olympics.com/tokyo-2020/en/games/tokyo-2020-playbooks/.

announced that it would strictly monitor the activities of foreign reporters via GPS. As expected, the International Federation of Journalists published a statement opposing this move.

§3. New Legislation Regarding Tokyo 2020

504. In relation to Tokyo 2020, the Act on the Promotion of Anti-Doping Activities in Sport was enacted as a new national law in October 2018, but no special law on ambush marketing and other matters was enacted. The Act on the Promotion of Anti-Doping Activities in Sport became the first domestic law to specify that doping practices were illegal, but the introduction of criminal penalties in the course of discussions on the enactment of the law was eventually postponed and no criminal penalties were imposed.

Selected Bibliography

The following books and publications are all in Japanese.

Abe, Tamaki. *Why Does Baseball Betting and Match-Fixing Not Go Away?*. Tokyo: KK Bestsellers Ltd., September 2010.

Chiba, Masaji & Hamano, Yoshio (eds). *An Introduction to Sports Law.* Tokyo: Taiiku Shisetsu Shuppan Ltd., December 1995.

Dai-ichi Tokyo Lawyers Association Comprehensive Law Research Institute Sports Law Research Team. *Legal Practice on Sports Rights and Disciplinary Sanctions – Appropriate Disciplinary Sanctions Against Athletes in the Era of Basic Sports Act*. Tokyo: Seibunsha, 2013.

Dougauchi, Masato. *A Consideration and Summary of the Main Points Concerning the First Three Years of the Japan Sports Arbitration Agency.* In *Towards Further Development in Sports Arbitration*, Tokyo: Sophia Law School, March 2006.

Dougauchi, Masato & Hayakawa, Yoshihisa (eds). *An Introduction to Sports Law.* Kyoto: Minerva Shobou Ltd., April 2011.

Doushisha Sports Policy Forum (ed.). *Sports Law and Policy.* Kyoto: Minerva Shobou Ltd., April 2001.

Gunji, Sadanori. *The Business Behind High School Baseball.* Tokyo: Chikumashobou Ltd., March 2008.

Harada, Munehiko. *Sports Industry Debate*. 4th edn. Tokyo: Kyourin-Shoin Ltd., May 1995.

Harada, Munehiko & Ogasawara, Etsuko (eds). *Sports Management.* Tokyo: Taishuukan Shoten Ltd., November 2008.

Hayakawa, Takehiko. *The Globalization of Sports and Media and Business: Sports Industry Course.* Tokyo: Soubunkikaku Ltd., February 2006.

Higuchi, Yoshio (ed.). *Professional Baseball Economics.* Tokyo: Nippon Hyoronsha Co., Ltd., September 1993.

Hirose, Ichirou (ed.). *Sports MBA.* Tokyo: Soubunkikaku Ltd., June 2006.

Hitotsubashi University Institute of Innovative Research (ed.). *Hitosubashi Business Review 2009 SPR* 56, no. 4 (Tokyo: Toyo Keizai Inc., March 2009).

Ito, Takashi. et al. *Sports Legal Consultation.* Tokyo: Seirinshorin Ltd., October 2000.

Japan Sports Arbitration Agency. *Sports Governance Guidebook for the Trouble Free Operation of Sports Associations*. Tokyo: Japan Sports Arbitration Agency, March 2011.

JEB Entertainment Co., Ltd. *10th Seminar on Supporting Players in the Football Business. DVD.* Tokyo: JEB Entertainment Co., Ltd., February 2011.

Selected Bibliography

Kamiya, Sounosuke. *Sports Law.* Tokyo: Sanseido Publishing Co., Ltd., October 2005.

Kawai, Keiji. *A Consideration of the Japan Professional Baseball Players Association's Strike – The Legal Rights of Professional Baseball Players. Legal Classroom* 2004, no. 291 (Tokyo: Yuhikaku Publishing Co., Ltd., 2004).

Kawai, Keiji & Wong, M. Glenn. *Law and Culture of Sports Business – U.S. and Japan*. Tokyo: Seibundo, 2012.

Kimura, Kichiji. *An Introduction to the History of Physical Education and Sport.* 2nd edn. Tokyo: Ichimura Publishing House, March 2010.

Maeda, Masahide (eds), et al. *Commentaries to the Penal Code.* 2nd edn. Tokyo: Koubundo Publishers Inc., 2007.

Masumoto, Yoshirou. *Show Me the Money: Legal Issues Concerning American Sports Agents*. Tokyo: Sony Magazines Inc., November 2011.

Nakajima, Takanobu. *Sumo Wrestling Economics.* Tokyo: Chikumashobo Ltd., March 2008.

Ogasawara, Masaru (ed.), et al. *An Introductory Dialogue to Sports Jurisprudence.* Tokyo: Fumashoubo Ltd., May 2005.

Ogasawara, Masaru (ed.), et al. *An Introductory Dialogue to Sports Jurisprudence.* 2nd edn. Tokyo: Fumashoubo Ltd., April 2007.

Ogasawara, Masaru & Suwa, Nobuo (eds). *Sports Risk Management.* Tokyo: Gyosei Corporation, September 2009.

Okamoto, Katsuhide. *Issues in Relation to the Taxation of Entertainment Corporations. National Tax College Research Papers*. 1987, 18 (Tokyo: National Tax Agency, 1987).

Okushima, Takayasu. *Nippon Professional Baseball Agreement and Antitrust Law. Jurist* 1993, no. 1032 (Tokyo Yuhikaku Publishing Co., Ltd., 1993).

Sasakawa Sports Foundation. *Sports Paper: The Future Direction for Sports*. Tokyo: Sasakawa Sports Foundation, February 2011.

Sasakawa Sports Foundation. *The 2006 SSF White Book on Sports*. Tokyo: Sasakawa Sports Foundation, March 2006.

Sasakawa Sports Foundation. *The 2010 SSF National Sporting Survey: Sports Life Data 2010*. Tokyo: Sasakawa Sports Foundation, December 2010.

Sawano, Masahiko. *The Glory and Frustration of Corporate Sports.* Tokyo: Seikyusha Ltd., June 2005.

Sports Trouble Specialist Team (ed.). *Q & A Sports Law Issues.* (revised ed.). Tokyo: Minjihou Kenkyuukai, November 2003.

Study Committee on Good Governance in Sports. *Sports Governance Practice Guide – Good Governance Study Group in Sports*. Tokyo: Minjiho-Kenkyukai, June 2014.

Suwa, Nobuo et al. *Contemporary Issues in Sports Policy.* Tokyo: Nippon Hyoronsha Co., Ltd, April 2008.

Suzuki, Shu. *Student Athletes: Special Admission on the Sport Quota and Duties under the Educational Agreement. The Legal Problems Facing Amateur Sports*, Annual Review 9 (Tokyo: Japan Sports Law Association, December 2002).

Tamaki, Masayuki. *What Are Sports?*. Tokyo: Kodansha Ltd., August 1999.

Uchiumi, Kazuo. *Pro Sports Debate: Pioneers of Sports Culture.* Tokyo: Soubunkikaku Ltd., March 2004.

Urakawa, Michitaro et. al. (ed.). *Standard Text – Sports Law.* Tokyo: Eidell Institute, 2016.

Ushiki, Sokiichiro. *The Temporary Employment Contracts of Corporate Sports Athletes.* Tokyo: Journal of the Japan Sports Law Association, 2002.

Yamazaki, Takuya & Ishiwatari, Shinsuke. *The Process of Introducing the Professional Baseball Agent System: The Status of the Implementation and Future Players Expectations: And the Fight to Introduce the System and Future Issues. Liberty & Justice* 2001, September Issue (Tokyo: Japan Federation of Bar Associations, 2001).

Yamazaki, Takuya. *Professional Baseball and Football Players' Rights and the Role of Lawyers in Japan. Liberty & Justice* 2009, August Issue (Tokyo: Japan Federation of Bar Associations, 2009).

Selected Bibliography

Index

The numbers here refer to paragraph numbers.

Amateurism, 1, 14, 197–206, 213–220, 229, 230
Ambush marketing, 392, 437, 438, 504
Anti-monopoly Act, 69, 280, 281, 292, 464–466, 468–471, 473, 474, 478, 479, 481–483, 485–488
B-league, 1, 10, 49, 317–318, 489, 495

Black Mist Scandal, 118, 120, 136–141
Broadcasting rights, 182, 388, 389, 391, 392, 394, 420–428
BSA, 15–18, 21–27, 54, 154, 157, 158, 160, 161, 195

CAS, 175, 176, 192, 193, 376, 384, 499
Copyright, 388, 390, 421, 430–434, 442, 453, 458

Discrimination, 83, 498
Draft (systems), 13, 265, 271–285, 291, 310, 465, 470, 473–474

Egawa Incident, 13, 280, 465

FIFA, 64, 74, 132, 266, 311–314, 316, 327, 329, 330, 344, 355, 401, 402, 437, 439, 446
FIFPro, 74, 315
Free agents, 81, 287, 289, 297–299, 304, 338

Gambling, 11, 117–130, 145, 147, 150
see also Public gambling
Ganaha Incident, 192, 356, 384

IOC, 368, 452, 497, 498, 502, 503
Image rights, 58–74, 266, 322, 325, 364, 422, 440–445, 457, 458, 460, 468, 469, 481–483

JADA, 185, 369, 370, 373–376, 384
JSPO, 33, 46, 48, 78, 115, 173, 174, 179, 185, 186, 190, 195, 368, 370
JFA, 33, 64, 65, 73, 74, 82, 203, 314, 327, 327–330, 349, 350–352, 355, 401, 405
JFTC, 69, 246, 285, 319, 465, 467, 471, 479, 480, 483, 487, 488
J-League, 1, 4, 10, 49, 73, 82, 132–135, 163, 192, 193, 269, 310, 313, 315, 321, 323, 341–343, 348, 351–356, 373, 384, 405, 406, 423, 434, 446, 489, 490, 494
JOC, 33, 46, 48, 61, 62, 173, 174, 179, 185, 186, 190, 195, 365, 369
JPBPA, 63, 68, 70, 71, 149, 202, 256, 257, 285, 289, 306, 327–330, 332, 335–337, 477
JPFA, 64, 73, 74, 258, 315, 316, 355
Japan Sports Agency, 45, 54
JSAA, 54, 159, 161, 173–181, 185, 188–196, 220, 223, 376, 384
JSC, 133, 134

Konami, 69, 70, 482, 483

Match-fixing, 52, 117–130, 135–153
Merchandising rights, 446–456
METI, 45, 128
MEXT, 22, 32, 33, 44, 45, 52, 54, 131, 133, 156, 157, 159, 194, 318, 370
MHLW, 45, 237, 243
MLB, 67, 71, 270, 282–287, 290, 294, 296–306, 383, 396
MLBPA, 67, 70, 306, 328, 336

National Sports Festival, 77, 78, 195, 370

Index

NPB, 475–480

Olympics, 15, 33, 46, 48–57, 61, 175, 176, 318, 365, 368, 371, 373, 446, 489, 496–504

Public gambling, 117, 118, 121, 126–130, 145

Reserve system, 265, 268, 270, 286–295, 310, 334, 338, 473–474

Sponsorship rights, 388, 435–439
Sports rights, 15–24, 37–43

Supreme Court, 35, 76, 102, 110, 167, 449

Tokyo District Court, 98–100, 112, 116, 168, 171, 205, 257, 386, 460
Tokyo High Court, 430
Toto, 117, 132
Trademarks, 390, 402, 436, 438, 439, 442, 447, 448, 452, 455, 456, 458

UNESCO, 20, 184, 185, 370

WADA, 365, 369, 374, 375, 377–379, 384

Yamaoka Scandal, 141–142

www.ingramcontent.com/pod-product-compliance
Lightning Source LLC
LaVergne TN
LVHW021111300926
849160LV00009B/696

* 9 7 8 9 4 0 3 5 4 8 9 1 3 *